P9-CIU-957

Against School Reform

(And in Praise of Great Teaching)

Against
School Reform
(And in Praise of
Great Teaching)

PETER S. TEMES

Ivan R. Dee

CHICAGO 2002

Library of Congress Cataloging-in-Publication Data:

Temes, Peter S., 1966–

   Against school reform (and in praise of great teaching) / Peter S. Temes.

     p. cm.

   Includes bibliographical references and index.

   ISBN 1-56663-481-4 (alk. paper)

    1. Educational change—United States. 2. Teachers—United States. I. Title.

LA217.2 .T45 2002

371.1'00973—dc21   2002067385

This book is for Judy Temes,

who has managed to teach me and tolerate me

for almost twenty years

Acknowledgments

BOTH MY PARENTS, Lloyd Temes and Roberta Lyons, were teachers, and gave me a strong sense of the nobility of the teacher's calling. My grandfather, Irving Rempell, has been a teacher all his life as a union organizer and activist, though he has never had a classroom. This book was inspired by Roberta, Lloyd, and Irving.

Marly Rusoff and Ilan Stavans gave me great encouragement early on in this project, and I owe them both great thanks.

Bill Murphy at Lynn English High School, Shirley Spielman at P.S. 195, Milton Kessler at SUNY Binghamton, and Robert Oprandy at Columbia University gave me glimpses of what great teachers can do.

Sam Freedman's book *Small Victories* is perhaps the greatest model I've had at hand for writing about schools, and all of James Herndon's books sit on my most revered bookshelf.

Lew Smith, Joe Coulson, Garth Katner, Judy Temes, and Dan

Acknowledgments

Born have been warm and challenging colleagues as I wrote this book.

Sandy Reeves at *Education Week*, Paula Dragosh at the *Chronicle of Higher Education*, Daniel Asa Rose at the *Forward*, and Jane Karr at the *New York Times* have given my work outlets while I wrote this book, and helped me imagine myself as a real writer. Judy Temes, Maria Russo, Bill Roorbach, and Ilan Stavans have kept me fueled by jealousy as their work has continued to set the highest standards of accomplishment. My deepest thanks to all.

The quotation from the *New York Times* about Donna Moffett is from "'S' Is for Satisfactory, Not for Satisfied," *New York Times*, July 1, 2001.

Quotations from Rexford Brown are drawn from his book *Schools of Thought: How the Politics of Literacy Shape Thinking in the Classroom*, published by Jossey-Bass in 1991.

The quotation from Jean Anyon is from her book *Ghetto Schooling: A Political Economy of Urban Educational Reform*, published by Teachers College Press in 1997.

The quotation from Martin Luther King's "Letter from Birmingham City Jail" is collected in *Why We Can't Wait*, published by Harper & Row in 1964.

The quotation from Esmé Raji Codell is taken from her book *Educating Esmé: Diary of a Teacher's First Year*, published by Algonquin Books in 2001.

Quotations from Judy Logan are drawn from her book *Teaching Stories*, published by Kodansha in 1997.

The quotation from Lew Smith is from his article "What Are

Schools For?," which appeared in *Education Week*, October 3, 2001.

The sample question from the Wheelock College test may be found on the college web site: http://www.wheelock.edu.

The Bank Street College "Credo" may be found on the college web site: http://www.bankstreet.edu.

Andy Baumgartner's quotation may be found in "Bob Chase's Column" for March 26, 2000, on the National Education Association web site: http://www.nea.org.

Contents

Against School Reform

(And in Praise of Great Teaching)

1

The State of
Our Schools,
and the Big Lie of
School Reform

Miss Whitman was doing just about everything wrong. She interrupted her fourth-grade students as they answered her questions. She did not stick to her announced lesson plans. She gave assignments and then changed her mind when students were halfway done with the work. It was easy to imagine a school administrator standing in the back of the classroom with a clipboard, noting her many slips and stumbles.

But she was a fabulous teacher. Kids lit up when she spoke to them, and you could watch them scrunch up their faces as they thought—and thought hard—when she asked them questions.

Just about all her students and their parents knew it too. She had a big heart. She loved the unexpected and welcomed nutty ideas from her fourth-graders, showing how their thoughts could be nudged toward whatever subjects the class was officially studying.

She worked without a model of reform for her classroom. She worked without a master plan or a mission statement. But she was a talented teacher, a smart person who enjoyed new ideas, enjoyed the company of young people, and had an instinctive respect for what other people thought and said. These were qualities she could never pick up in a book or a training class, but they made her the great teacher she was.

Miss Whitman is a prime example of the most important rule in education: a great teacher is more important than anything else. Consider the terrible physical conditions that many students in poor neighborhoods endure in their schools—but then think about what one great teacher can do with a circle of kids sitting on the grass, without even a school building to their name. Think about what a great teacher can do with a class of thirty students that a poor—or just plain average—teacher cannot do with a class of twenty. Think about what a great teacher can do with outdated teaching methods, that a mediocre teacher cannot do with the best brain-engineered methods fresh from the research laboratory. Teaching, after all, is an interaction between people, between teachers and learners.

The externals of school structure cannot guarantee a teacher's success, though they can stack the deck against a teacher. At their best, well-structured schools get out of the talented teacher's way. At the other end of the spectrum, schools that make their own institutional presence heavily felt diminish the power of the individual teacher to do the hard work of real education. Unfortunately the large majority of the efforts to improve education in America in the past two decades have emphasized school structure and the nature of our institutions, rather than the power of great teachers to teach, and the need for great schools quietly to support those teachers. But it's never too late. Teachers, parents, and students can make a major difference in their schools by learning to appreciate and support the power of great teaching, and by helping the institutional presence of schools to step into the background while the spotlight shines on teachers and students.

The key is to focus less on reforming the institutions and more on supporting the individuals who teach. Radical change *will* come to schools if great teachers get the support they need, but by focusing on great teachers the change will be bottom-up and highly customized to the real situations of specific schools and classrooms. This is the kind of change that lasts.

FIRST, DO NO HARM

Physicians swear to the Hippocratic Oath, affirming that they will dedicate themselves to the health of their patients above all else—above money, above politics, and above power. Education professionals—particularly school board members, school administrators, and policymakers—would do the world a great service by taking a similar pledge. The very first words of the doctor's oath are a promise to "First, do no harm." This would be a great first step for schools. If American schools did nothing more than stop making life more difficult for teachers who want to teach and students who want to learn, we'd all be a lot better off.

15

And they can. American schools can do a much better job of supporting teachers and students. The first step is to change the emphasis in the broad debates, the big grants, and the education business overall from school reform to teacher support.

There's an old joke that goes a long way toward explaining why we have such an emphasis today on fixing the problems of schools—which are, after all, merely *mechanisms* to deliver education, not to be confused with *actual education*—rather than fixing the more abstract interactions between teachers and students that are education itself. A man loses a diamond ring in his living room. One moment he's gazing intently at the diamond, and the next it rolls off his palm and somewhere onto the floor. A quick look around the floor reveals nothing—it is lost. His friend stops by to say hello, sizes up the situation, and offers to help. "Thanks," says the man. "Let's get to work looking in the kitchen." "The kitchen?" his friend asks. "Why look in the kitchen? You lost your ring in the living room." "But look," says the man, "the light here in the living room is so dim. We'll never find it in here. The light in the kitchen is so much brighter."

The unfortunate fact is that many of the billions of dollars and millions of hours spent on school reform in the United States in the past decade have gone to the well-lit places of education, the places where reform efforts are easiest to observe and applaud, though the real work of education lies elsewhere. What needs most fixing in American schools are the dimly lit corners, the "soft" elements of learning that have to do with the magic of a great teacher—the qualities that Miss Whitman has that are so hard to measure. When we spend our time and money on the measurable things—"time on task," test scores, and the structure of curriculum—we can do some good, but what the teacher brings to the class matters far more. Miss Whitman is a great teacher because of her raw belief in her students, her overall outlook on kids and education, her love of being surprised. These are small-scale, idiosyncratic qualities. They can be cultivated, supported, and celebrated at the local level, teacher by teacher, but are almost impossible to address at a distance. And, unfortunately, most school reform efforts are crafted at some distance from the classroom.

People who approach school reform as citizens, motivated by the general feeling that our schools should be better, often address the abstract, system-level problems because their own motives are abstract. A fellow I know in California puts it this way: "Schools need help, sure. Teachers I'm sure need help too. But I'm more interested in the system, the higher-level view. I can do some good using my expertise in business and planning by trying to make changes in the bigger systems, and I'm all for others getting down and dirty and making change at the local level if that's what they want to do." This is a reasonable-seeming proposition, and without a doubt the "higher-level" systems of our schools need a lot of fixing. But I question what good this kind of fixing does for individual students.

Trying to fix schools from the top down means grappling with the slippery and skillful self-defenses of the bureaucracy itself—working with organization charts, handbooks of procedures, the habits and behaviors of literally thousands of functionaries in the school system. And all that work, every redrafting of a policy, every session to explain new procedures to rooms filled with administrators, does little or nothing to touch students directly. Only if the high-level change actually takes effect, and reaches down to the school buildings and classrooms—and then, only if that change lasts—will students feel any real difference.

What makes for lasting change? Support throughout an organization—at the bottom as well as the top. So why not start at the ground level, with individual teachers? Yes, the Byzantine procedures of many school bureaucracies need to be changed. But why not change them by first offering more support for individual teachers to experiment in their classrooms, to do more of what they feel makes their classrooms lively and spontaneous, and less that hooks them into the larger machine of the school system? Bureaucracies feed on attention, even the negative attention that comes with reform efforts. But they shrivel by being made unnecessary, by being circumvented. They are best reformed not by being laid out and operated upon but by being replaced with more efficient and humane alternatives. And those alternatives are constantly being invented at the ground level. Teachers create ways to circumvent ugly aspects of the system every day, though these small innovations are generally kept from view, lest they be discovered and quashed. If we use our resources to identify and encourage better alternatives to existing policies and practices, we can lay the groundwork for fixing the high-level problems in our schools while touching teachers and students directly, right from the outset. We can improve their classrooms through the very process of change, rather than merely hoping that once reform has run its course, positive change will trickle down from the system into the classroom.

JOY AND RISK

Many teachers—in my experience, not a majority but an important number—manage to teach with something approaching joy, though always with some risk. The risk comes from the many forces within most school systems that push toward uniformity, simplicity, and control, even when these qualities demand the sacrifice of the spark of the unexpected that animates effective education. Consider, for example, the story of one of New York City's fresh teaching recruits, Donna Moffett, who began teaching in the city schools in 2000. Moffett took a large pay cut to become a teacher, leaving a career as a paralegal. But she loves to teach. She completed her first year emotionally drained but exhilarated. A feature about Moffett in the *New York Times* tells a bit of her story, including her challenges within the New York City school system:

> Colleagues and superiors have complained about her style, which can lean toward eccentric, and instructed her to adhere to a stricter, more no-nonsense routine. In her latest rebellion, she wrote as much as she could fit in the comment box on each student's report card, despite advice from veterans to "keep it brief."
>
> In an effort to praise one boy who was at the bottom of the class academically, she wrote, "He is very observant and expressive, as well as kind and loving and helpful." And she described a girl who could never stop chattering as "full of joy and cheerful expression."

"Maybe one could make the argument that I am too emotionally involved," she said. "But each of these children is so complex. To say something as simple as 'doing well' or 'good luck' just doesn't cut it."

Ms. Moffett's approach could backfire at a time when the charge to buck up inner-city schools with standardized, back-to-basics curriculums is increasingly popular. But Ms. Moffett believes that while she has miles to go to become a good teacher, the style she has adopted in this first year will carry her far.

Moffett's instincts take her in two important directions—first, to have more dialogue with her students, to give them more rather than less; and second, to experiment. Perhaps longer comments won't help. But she wants to try out an idea that feels best for her and for her students. Her supervisors and veteran teachers push in the other direction—say less to your students, do things the tried-and-true way. Even if Moffett's instincts prove wrong and there is some hidden virtue in summing up a student's year with two casual words rather than a warm paragraph, the very fact that she is trying something new, taking a risk on an approach that she believes in, will make Moffett try a little harder. That is the cardinal value of experiment and innovation: not only that new ideas might be better than the old, but that in the process of trying to find out, people commit greater energy and concern to the work at hand. Experimenters do generally try harder and care more than the caretakers of the tried and true.

Energy and caring go beyond the immediate; they become habits, a way of working. Imagine, for example, what would happen if Moffett was forced to teach for a day using the methods a supervisor designed for her, following the educational philosophy of "keep it brief," while the same supervisor was forced to teach using Moffett's more expressive and expansive approach. Even though I think Moffett's specific practices are better, I'd rather have my children taught by Moffett herself, using just about any methods at all. Her conviction that students are worth more than two words, and her inclination to experiment and commit herself to trying new things, will rise above the specifics of how a classroom exercise is structured. And, alas, I would dread to see the paragraphs of forced warmth her supervisor would churn out under protest while dreaming of the older, easier ways of doing things.

FROM THE CITY TO THE COUNTRY

Moffett's experience reveals a broken system's local effects: the influence of teachers and administrators who have adapted to the system's weaknesses with a philosophy of instruction that is frighteningly well summarized in the phrase "Keep it brief." The story of Dennis Littky makes a similar point. Littky was a celebrated big-city junior high school principal looking to change his life. He moved to a small New Hampshire town, expecting to earn a modest living writing and doing odd jobs. Inevitably he was drawn back to life in school. His town's schools were obviously failing. Most school days, students lined the main street loafing and smoking well into the evening. Few high school graduates went on to college. At the height of the school system's problems, one local citizen said to a school board member in a public meeting, "You owe us an explanation." The board member replied, "I don't owe you anything," and led the board into a closed-door session.

Littky applied for the high school principal's job and got it when the board's first choice rejected the job because of its low salary. Littky turned the school around, becoming a hero of the students and the town. Then the school board fired him for being unorthodox and showing them too little respect. Littky's story has a happy ending, though. Following town-wide protest and a number of formal appeals, he won his job back and stayed as principal for a decade. The school district's leadership clearly made bad decisions and was widely known to be ineffectual at best and destructive at worst. The board's antics and Littky's success in dealing with them eventually became the basis of a successful book (*Teacher*) and television movie, celebrating one small victory in the struggle to fix broken schools. Often overlooked, though, is the wisdom of Littky's strategy. He did not begin his work by trying to change the school board, bad as it was, or any of the other district-wide issues that touched his school. Instead he set out to make the classroom experience of his students better by supporting his classroom teachers. He understood that lasting change had to begin there, and he was right. Later the board fell of its own weight. Littky became a hero and rallying point for the board's opposition because *he had already succeeded* in the classroom. No one could argue against that success and win, though many tried.

These examples should help us answer a number of fundamental questions about school reform. How much money and time should we devote to fixing high-level policies and procedures? How much of our effort should go, at first blush, to re-training or replacing administrators and policymakers like the un-caring school board member in New Hampshire? How much, instead, should go to support Donna Moffett and teachers like her? Do we begin to make change at the top, with the functionar-ies, the system-wide programs, and the overall structure of school systems, or do we begin with the experience of the individual teacher and the individual student, and push the change up?

Should we put our efforts as citizens into the political chal-lenge of unseating the local school board in a small New Hamp-shire town (hoping, of course, that their replacements will be better, the kind of hope that is often unfulfilled)? Or, as our first order of business, should we follow Dennis Littky's example and circumvent the boards, commissions, and committees and go right to the classroom to begin improving what goes on there?

Why choose? Because if we don't, the inertia of large school systems will choose for us, and resources will be sucked to the top of these systems. Systematic change is, of course, vital, but to begin at the system level is a mistake for two reasons. First, be-cause the value of change becomes "back loaded." The process of putting the change in place does not really help teachers and stu-dents; we ask them to wait until the system has changed, and then benefit from the changes. But ground-level change is by defi-nition "front loaded." When school improvement begins not with politics and large programs but with what teachers do in their classrooms every day, the minute the process of change begins, students and teachers benefit. Given that so many large-scale school improvement projects never officially reach completion anyway, how could we possibly choose the all-or-nothing mindset of system-wide reform over the hands-on realities of making change by helping teachers teach better one classroom at a time? Yet efforts at top-down change absorb the vast majority of school reform dollars and hours.

WHAT ONLY TEACHERS CAN DO

In 1993 the book *Schools of Thought* told the story of one Southern state that had spent ten years on top-down, statewide reform efforts, with a special emphasis on improving students' ability to read and write. Here's what Rexford G. Brown, the author, had to say at the end of a chapter summing up years of observation of dozens of schools:

> I can only observe what this chapter's glimpses of our visits suggest: that none of the school-reform initiatives, with the possible exception of establishing . . . kindergarten, has yet changed the way students and teachers read, write, talk, and think. In other words, no reform has penetrated to the heart of the literacy question.
>
> The State has reorganized departments, changed educational appointments, set up programs, added personnel, lowered various ratios, created more tests, strengthened compulsory-attendance laws, improved certification requirements, developed new procedures for performance evaluation, trained people in instructional management, raised graduation requirements, offered more scholarships, mandated new studies of school organization, and raised teachers' salaries. States can do these things. But

can they change what really matters—how people read, write, talk with each other, how they discover and wrestle with ideas, how they strengthen, broaden, and deepen their literacy?

Brown's question has a definite answer. Can states—or school superintendents, or federal education policies—change the way people read, write, think, and talk? Of course not. That change, when it does happen, comes from inspired teachers.

Jean Anyon, in her book *Ghetto Schools*, points out the particular need in the poorest schools for a more sensible approach to fixing them. She lays bare the fact that top-down reform has simply not worked for these schools. "Why," she asks,

with such a large percentage of urban institutions reporting restructuring activity, has the picture of education in inner cities not brightened considerably? In the last 15 years Boston, Chicago, Cincinnati, Cleveland, Dade County, Detroit, Hammond, Louisville, New York, Philadelphia, Pittsburgh, and Rochester, New York—among other cities— have been in the news for their attempts to make city schools more successful for low-income students by using a variety of restructuring activities. This most recent wave of reform, of course, follows close on the heels of several decades of other educational reforms in urban districts: federal programs in the late 1960s and early 1970s, and the decades of accountability and standards reforms in the 1970s, 1980s, and 1990s. . . . The latest wave of reform, of which restructuring is a component, is referred to by advocates as "systematic reform." Activity to produce systematic change is an attempt to pull together disparate types of reform from the past several decades, and to overcome contradictory initiatives generated by different levels of the education system. Given the dismal state of schooling in most of our central cities, however, it seems clear that this recent wave of educational reform has not succeeded there.

This view, summed up in Anyon's simple statement that "educational reform has not succeeded," is almost universal among classroom teachers, who are more likely to see value in practical things—like a little more money for supplies or more time to work with students one-on-one—than in large-scale models for reform.

An *Education Week* article from November 2001 tells the story of the Memphis, Tennessee, school system's discovery that top-down reform does not work after an enormously expensive commitment to large-scale reform. "When the superintendent in Memphis, Tenn., announced he was scuttling that district's long-running effort to install school-wide improvement programs in every school in the city," the article began,

> the decision seemed unusual enough to merit national attention. But the July closing of the city's closely watched experiment was just the latest in a string of setbacks in the nationwide movement known as comprehensive or "whole school" reform.
>
> Since 1998, districts in San Antonio and Miami–Dade County have abandoned some efforts to adopt well-known, "off the shelf" improvement models on a large scale. Early reports from New Jersey, where 30 poor districts are under a

1998 court order to adopt schoolwide improvement models, also suggest that implementation in that state, while still on track, is running into obstacles and pockets of resistance.

The obstacles and resistance might be overcome in New Jersey. Or, like Memphis, like San Antonio, like Miami, like New York, like Baltimore—the list is endless—New Jersey just might discover that top-down change cannot accomplish what teachers, working from the ground up, can.

Perhaps all this feels too cynical, too negative about high-level school change. Yet the stories of two particular schools I recently learned about keep me from warming toward reform programs even at the single-school level.

"BRING ME A HURRICANE"

I learned about these schools when I was on a panel of judges at a large university in New York that runs a program to recognize the best school-change programs around the country. We looked over the case studies of a few dozen schools that had been nominated as outstanding examples of school reform. Two of the winning schools stood out for me. One was a middle school in Florida, the other was a grade school in Boston.

The school in Florida sat across the street from an air force base. Not far away, a public housing project provided homes for about two hundred families. The children of the air base staff were truly a mixed lot. Their parents were pilots, mechanics, and other military staff. They represented every ethnic and geographic origin. Because all their families were connected to the military, they all had steady income. The children from the public housing project were mostly African American and Hispanic, and poor. The student body overall was tremendously varied, with students performing at all academic levels. Then came a major hurricane. The air base was evacuated early and the military children pulled from school. The base was leveled by the storm, and the school was devastated as well. The school was eventually rebuilt, but the air base was shut down for good. When the school reopened, fewer than one-third of the students from before the storm remained—and just about all of them were from the housing project. With lower levels of enrollment, the school lost most of its teaching staff, and soon leaders of the school district recognized the crisis at hand. The school was rezoned to pull in students from other parts of town, and a magnet program was launched, allowing high-scoring students from neighboring towns to apply to attend special programs. Soon enough, enrollment was back up, the principal was able to hire new teachers, and test scores across the board began to rise—even higher than they had been when the air base was open. So the school was recognized as a model of effective school reform.

But was this really a story of one school reforming itself, or was it more a story of two distinct schools? Before the hurricane, the school had a certain population of students, a stable faculty, and a building that everyone recognized as their school. After the storm, the student population was largely different—not only different kids but kids coming from different neighborhoods and towns. The teaching staff was almost entirely new, and the building itself was new. The school was, in fact, a different place, populated by different people. There were very few lessons that another school could take away and apply—short of calling in a hurricane to clear the decks, so that everyone could start from scratch with a new building, new teachers, and new kids.

A successful reform story goes more like this: a group of teachers, parents, and students comes together and transforms the lives they lead in school, without shuttling off the lower-scoring students or diluting them in a wave of higher-scoring kids from across town. These stories are few and far between, but they all center on what happens inside the individual classroom. It's harder to win awards for change that moves from the ground up, one classroom after another slowly improving, because there is no big new idea, no special system-wide or school-wide program, to rally around. The real answer to school reform is highly complex—as complex as a school full of idiosyncratic teachers all doing remarkable things in their own highly personal ways. How do you point a television camera at that? How do you capture that in a mission statement, or package it for replication throughout a large district? It can be done, of course, but slowly, from the ground up, and only when individual teachers of great talent and dedication become the heroes of school reform. The first step is to realize that enduring change lives with the teacher, and to begin looking for teachers already doing great things to celebrate. Time spent looking for whole schools doing great things is often wasted, because most school-wide success stories tend to be impossible to duplicate—like the hurricane school in Florida—or the result of structural change that has little to do with real improvements in education.

In the school-change award program, the other winning school that made a great impression on me sits in a low-income immigrant neighborhood in Boston. It exemplifies school change as a result of structural forces like population migration patterns. Change at that school had very little to do with its improved education; instead it was the result of students who test higher on standardized tests systematically replacing lower-scoring students in a given school.

The neighborhood is tough. After dark the wide streets are largely empty of people, though cars move through the neighborhood around the clock, many heading west to the suburbs at a steady pace, others slowing at corners to troll for drugs or prostitutes. But the neighborhood is far from desperate. The storefronts that line the main streets are active—small groceries, lunch-counter restaurants, video stores, and check-cashing operations provide a hum of economic life, and families are abundantly in evidence. Mothers with small children are out during the day, and whole families walk together in the early evenings. Families have moved here in groups; a block away, two blocks, many have relatives. And so the traffic of families who are out visiting gives the area an old-fashioned, settled feeling during daylight hours.

The families who live here are very poor and highly mobile. They tend to make their first American homes in the neighborhood, save money, and move to more solidly working-class parts of town. The mobility is so dramatic, in fact, that waves of immigrants come and go with regularity. Southeast Asians might make up the majority of the neighborhood for two or three years, and then a wave of Caribbean immigrants might come to predominate, or a few hundred families displaced by war, famine, or economic disaster in Eastern Europe, Western Africa, or South America. Each group brings with it a distinct set of cultural habits and strengths, and the local school takes on the character of its students and their families. During the 1990s families from rural areas in the Dominican Republic made up most of the neighborhood. Beginning in the late 1990s, though, a wave of families fleeing Bosnia's civil war settled there, and their children soon made up a substantial portion of the student body.

Most of the Dominican families had been farm workers in their home country, and their children had never attended school. Not only were most of them unable to read or write English, they were unable to read or write in their native language, Spanish. Their teachers had to teach them more than language; they had to teach them the very concept of literacy. And they did this well. The Dominican students learned, their families worked and saved, and they went off to new neighborhoods. Their test scores were not high, but a great deal of education took place in their classrooms.

The Bosnian students were different. Refugees from a brutal war, many brought a general sense of terror with them to school. But many of their parents had been professionals in their home country. They were poor—typical of new immigrants—but most of these students had completed at least a few years of schooling at home, so they would be more likely to work at a higher level once they had mastered rudimentary English. And that's exactly what happened. As the Bosnian students became a larger and larger presence at the school, average scores on standardized tests began to rise. At the same time any number of new programs were introduced, including extended hours for basic math instruction and school uniforms. Still, there was a direct cause-and-effect relationship to be seen: more students from better-educated families meant higher scores for the school. Were the higher scores a function of school reform? Forgive the skeptic who believes that the change in student population overwhelmed whatever impact the new school programs had.

These two school reform "success stories" are a kind of absurd extreme of the very idea of school reform. They make the case that even when efforts at reform seem to achieve strong results, things are not necessarily what they seem. And most school reform efforts do not produce the kind of measurable school-wide successes that these two schools demonstrated. In most cases, new programs produce a spark of energy and then fall back to the baseline that existed before they arrived.

CHANGE FROM WITHIN

Michael Bailin is president of the Edna McConnell Clark Foundation, an organization that has spent tens of millions of dollars to support school reform efforts in the United States over the last ten years. But Bailin has decided to take his foundation out of the school reform business. Why? Because he has concluded that school reform does not, in fact, work. "Even under the best of circumstances," he says, the institutional side of schools "can absorb or co-opt the energy of the reformers. "Institutions—particularly large, publicly funded institutions like our major school systems—are hard to change. They resist change with the mighty powers of entrenched bureaucrats. Most fiercely of all, they resist large-scale public change—the kinds of efforts that begin with public statements that things are bad and must be fixed. And this, of course, is precisely the language of modern school reform.

Large institutions are most vulnerable to change when it comes from within, and comes incrementally. Large institutions can be changed most effectively not by saying to them, "You're broken; I want to fix you," but by finding and supporting those inside the institutions who already have better ideas and are fighting the lonely fight to keep those ideas alive. Help those individuals—the spirited and gifted teachers within our bureaucratic schools—and real change has a fighting chance.

NOT A NEW PROBLEM

The urge to improve our schools has been with us since the very beginning of European settlement in North America, and earlier. More than two thousand years ago, Plato wrote that "the reformation of education is the great business of every man while he lives." And Horace Mann, the reformer whose hand is still quite evident in the shape of American schools, dedicated decades of his life in the mid-1800's to a crusade for what he called "a truer education."

The current era of school reform began in 1983 with the report of a blue-ribbon government panel titled *A Nation at Risk*. That report made two main points. The first was that Americans must compete with the educated citizens of many other nations, and that the standards for schooling in other nations seemed to be higher. The second point was less practical but perhaps even more important. It was about the core values of our nation:

The people of the United States need to know that
individuals in our society who do not possess the levels of

skill, literacy, and training essential to this new era will be effectively disenfranchised, not simply from the material rewards that accompany competent performance, but also from the chance to participate fully in our national life. A high level of shared education is essential to a free, democratic society and to the fostering of a common culture, especially in a country that prides itself on pluralism and individual freedom.

We have to improve our schools, the report said, to keep faith with our nation's fundamental commitment to individual liberty. If some citizens are offered excellent public schooling while others are offered schools that don't prepare them to think and act like free and independent people, we will be guilty of creating a servant class of Americans.

The first argument of *A Nation at Risk* is debatable. Yes, the average American student performs at a lower level than the average student in, say, Germany. But our schools are based on the democratic notion that *all* students should be prepared for higher education. Especially at higher grade levels, many students who would be diverted to trade schools in other nations remain in academic school programs in the United States. Their test scores are lower and pull down the averages. But our nation's commitment to social mobility and equal opportunity is well served by the practice of placing the large majority of students in academic schools, even if that results in lower average test scores overall.

The tests that compare students from various countries to one another would do the United States a service if they compared academic achievement not only of all students at set grade levels but of all children at certain ages. There is solid evidence to suggest that although the average German tenth-grader, for example, outscores her American counterpart in math and science, the average American fifteen-year-old will, in all likelihood, outscore the average German fifteen-year-old. Why? Because only about half of all German students are still on an academic track at the age of fifteen, while a much larger proportion of American students at that age are still being challenged with academic work. The Germans essentially screen out the students with lower math and science scores at an earlier age and divert them to trade schools. In our country, those students remain on the academic track because, as a matter of policy and philosophy, our educational system assumes that higher expectations for everyone is a better idea than screening out lower performers and expecting less of them.

The second point of *A Nation at Risk* is much harder to address but impossible to deny. The Declaration of Independence charts a course for this country based on the idea that we shall have no aristocracy. The powers and obligations of government shall rest, instead, with the people. In a nation ruled by a narrow caste, quality education is generally reserved for that caste—they will run the nation, so they must understand the practical and intellectual levers of power. But if the American people are to govern ourselves, we must educate ourselves—all of us—well. To the degree that we, as a nation, fail to provide all American children with excellent education, we are unworthy of our highest national ideals of self-government.

TODAY THERE IS NO CHOICE

Although this ideological argument for excellent schools has been with us for a very long time, we have never really risen to meet it. The poor children of this nation have never had schools consistently as fine as the schools given, free, to the wealthy. In the agricultural and industrial economies of the eighteenth and nineteenth centuries, this inequity was less obvious, and to the middle and upper classes less troubling, than it is in the emerging information- and service-based economy. In an agricultural economy the possession of productive land was the key to wealth, and productive land was largely a matter of inheritance. Those without land could generally earn subsistence wages working the land of others. Not much classroom learning was required. In the industrial era that extended through the years following World War II, wages tended to be even better for those without their own capital than they had been in agricultural days. Picture a young man, circa 1950, living in a small town in Ohio, feeling frustrated in school. At the age of sixteen, why not walk out of class and go across town to the steel mill, or the quarry, or the manufacturing plant? Physical strength and good work habits would be enough. A job, likely to pay well enough eventually to support a family (however meagerly), would require little more during the industrial era.

The image of a young person waking up in the morning with no more than the will to work, and going out to find that work with every prospect of success, is something we have lost. Will and strength are no longer enough. Today a combination of knowledge, the ability to learn, and "softer" communications skills is essential for the average citizen to head out in the morning and eventually come back with a job. All these qualifications take years to develop—years spent, when things happen as they should, in school. These are the gifts—knowledge, the ability to learn, and the ability to communicate comfortably with others—that excellent teachers give their students.

Most American children in the nineteenth century did not attend high school, and that was no barrier to them finding places (however miserable some of those places might have been) in the broader economy. Through the 1960s, if the average American student did not receive the kind of education he or she needed to go on to college, or to become a skilled learner and user of information, that was not a tragedy; alternatives awaited. Indeed, American industry relied on a workforce socially and intellectually prepared for the factory. Who else, after all, would take all those factory jobs? But today there is no choice. We must take up the challenge of equal education implied in the Declaration of Independence, and we must succeed, because today our economy has little room for citizens who have been poorly educated.

WE MUST TALK ABOUT TEACHING AND LEARNING

By most historical standards, our schools *are* better than they have ever been. While average classroom achievement may be down, the number of classrooms is up dramatically, and a far wider range of Americans is welcomed into our schools. The idea that schools are for every American child is a new one, particularly in the higher grades. Census data tell us that in 1900 only 11 percent of fourteen- to seventeen-year-olds were in school, while in the year 2000 that number was 93 percent. Thirteen percent of the adult population in 1900 were high school graduates; in 2000 that number was 83 percent. Teacher salaries in 1900 were stunningly low by today's standards—$328 was the average annual salary for a teacher in 1900. Adjusted for inflation, that comes to only $6,560 in 2001 dollars, compared to a national average of $40,600 today. Clearly the last century has seen important improvements in our schools.

But talking about schools in general will get us only so far. We must talk about education—the acts of teaching and learning—far more than we talk about schools. Teaching and learning, the essential collaboration of teachers and students, can be defined in many ways. In its essence, though, as more than one philosopher has said, education consists of a teacher at one end of a log and a student at the other, with books and words between them. That is probably just as useful a description of teaching and learning as any of the more complex alternatives to emerge from the education profession in the last few hundred years, and it captures well the fact that we are talking about real people here, real children and real adults.

The problems of American schools are generally discussed in the abstract. "Student performance" generally refers to hundreds or thousands or millions of students, not any child in particular, while "teacher preparedness" usually deals with the hundreds of teachers in a school district, or even the entire collection of three million public school teachers at work in the United States today. These are important issues, but the realities of education at the local level are far more important. The large, abstract issues of education in general mean nothing to the student stuck in a classroom with a poor teacher, just as they mean nothing to the teacher stuck in a school that rejects spontaneity and a spirit of discovery in the classroom. While signs of improvement in general may or may not make a difference to individual teachers and students, improvement in one classroom makes an incontrovertible difference for that teacher and those students. That certainty, that knowledge that change made close at hand is real, is much more valuable than the maybe so, maybe not impact of high-level school change. Education *as experienced by teachers and students*, rather than education measured in the aggregate, is the only sensible place to begin to make education in this country better.

Plato declared that a good teacher should be "the midwife of the student's ideas." This is a dramatic challenge to the way we teach in the United States today, educating large numbers of students in roughly uniform ways. In his own day, when teachers and students walked about in pairs, thinking and talking together, Plato's prescription to teachers was less heretical. Most important in Plato's definition of teaching is his immense respect for the student. The student, in his model, is not an empty vessel into which a teacher can pour knowledge. At the same time, though, the student is not seen as a teacher, nor as the teacher's equal. Plato does not abandon the obligations of authority, as some American reformers at times do. Instead Plato sees the teacher as having the obligation to teach, to be the student's superior in clear ways, but to take the student's ideas as the measure of the success of any lesson. There is a refreshing sense of honesty—intellectual and social—in this Platonic model of education. In my experience in

American schools today, the very best teachers manage to pre-serve Plato's vision of what a teacher can and should be, even in front of a room of thirty ten-year-olds.

For school change to succeed, efforts need to begin with the teacher. And for teachers to succeed, they must respond to their students' ideas, as Plato suggests. In every conventional class-room the teacher has skill and knowledge that the students do not. Those skills and that knowledge are why the teacher is the teacher—they make up the foundation of what the teacher has to teach. But that roomful of students has its own pool of ideas—less knowledge and skill than the teacher, most likely, but the kind of native genius and fresh perspectives that make children an endless source of creativity and hope. In every field, surprise is at the center of progress. The scientist begins an experiment with a notion of what may happen, but more important than that expec-tation is a keen attentiveness to *anything else* that may happen, be-cause most great discoveries are the result of surprises of one kind or another. And in music, in history, in literature—the list of sub-jects can go on—the familiar is made more significant when put in the context of the unexpected. Education is no exception. The greatest teachers are those who create rich opportunities for their students to think and say surprising things, and who have the presence of mind to celebrate original thinking. The very worst as-pect of many school reform programs is that they are preplanned and preprogrammed to reach narrowly prescribed outcomes. They do not encourage or reward the great surprises or the spirit of original thinking that can make education rise above the ordi-nary. They sacrifice Plato's individualistic emphasis on the student's ideas for the bureaucrat's emphasis on the teacher's performance. Much is lost in this shift.

THREE DO'S AND ONE DON'T

So, how can we support Miss Whitman and the many talented teachers like her? How can we be sure to hire them into our schools in the first place, and then keep them there for long, satisfying careers? This book is dedicated to three "do's" and one "don't" that answer these questions.

Emphasize Individuals. The first thing we have to do is understand the individual dynamics of great teaching. Teaching is a personal act, accomplished by individuals. We need to support and celebrate great teachers as individuals, rather than continuing in our cultural habit of addressing education as a mass endeavor.

Year after year, pollsters report that when asked about the quality of public schools in the United States, most people think that schools in general are pretty bad—but that the schools they and their own children have attended are pretty good. Another way of putting this is to say that, on average, people think their own schools are okay but that other people's schools are in trouble.

While there is no question at all that our schools need to be improved, by many measures they are doing better today than ten, twenty, and thirty years ago. The qualifications of teachers are higher, class sizes are smaller (nationally, they have gone down on average from 22.3 students per teacher in 1970 to 18.9 in the mid-nineties, according to the U.S. Department of Education), and many more students once pushed out of academic programs are now in the mainstream. Most Americans see this progress when they look at the schools close at hand; they don't manage to see it when they look at the abstract notion of "American education" in general.

The closer we are to things, after all, the better our judgment of them. Like the old slogan "Think globally, act locally," the impulse to get into a single classroom to help an individual teacher—and to support the general principle that teachers should be free to innovate in their classrooms—is full of wisdom. The diffuse anxiety of ordinary people about schools in general too often leads to diffuse actions to help schools in general. Perhaps some good comes of this, but there is no question that practical, local, concrete actions to make things better close at hand do real and enduring good. So don't ask, "How can I help America's schools improve?" Instead, go to the school nearest your home and ask the first teacher you can get your hands on, "How can I help you today?"

Keep It Real. Second, we need to remind everyone involved in the teaching profession what John Dewey said clearly several decades ago: education is not preparation for life; it is life itself. Teachers who teach the history of democracy by lecturing and enforcing top-down discipline show their students that undemocratic practice trumps democratic ideals, at least in their classrooms. What the teacher does as a person matters. How the teacher relates to students, how the classroom is structured, and the kinds of questions the teacher brings to students all present to students a set of values that the teacher uses to keep the classroom working. This is not to say that all classrooms should be models of democracy; students are, after all, students and not yet full citizens. But teachers should be models of honest, thoughtful communication. This is the second "do": ensure that teachers relate to students honestly and thoughtfully. Put another way, the idea is for teachers to keep their interactions with students *real*. Teachers who connect with their classes by reading from scripts of old lesson plans or by asking questions that have only preconceived right and wrong answers feel false to most students, and for good reason. These teachers aren't offering the kind of spontaneous, honest interaction that people generally recognize as normal, respectful behavior. This kind of rehearsed talk proceeds without much interaction at all in fact—it's all talk and little or no listening, not a good plan for making an impression on young minds. And teachers do need to listen to students, not because students know more than teachers do (they don't), not because students should control the classroom (they shouldn't), but because in school as everywhere else, listening is a sign of respect. It reaffirms the notion that the teacher, in addition to being older and wiser than the students, is also a part of the social world of the school. To deny that the teacher lives on the same social plane as the students is to lose innumerable teaching opportunities, sacrificed to ideals of articifiality that lead teachers to withhold when they should reach out. Keeping it real means not pretending that the teacher has nothing to learn. It means emphasizing the excitement of learning—the teacher alongside the student—rather than the formalities of social power.

Make It New. The third "do" is to experiment, all the time. Spend a day in a school and you'll be impressed with how unpredictable every moment is. Spend a decade in a school and you

43

might find that the practice of teaching the same subjects to children of the same age time and time again becomes routine to the point of exhaustion. Most teachers are, after all, civil servants. They are relatively small players in immense government entities. And so they face a choice—allow the larger institutional forces of sameness and bureaucracy to set the tone, or focus on the smaller-scale interactions and surprises that make up the minutes and hours of the teacher's day. The biology teacher who solves the big problem of how to teach cell division—not just today but for years to come, forever, by writing a lesson plan that will cover the bases without fail—misses the opportunity to see the problem as a new, small-scale challenge every time a class approaches it. The challenge, after all, is not the *teaching* of cell division but the *learning* of it by a wild variety of individual students who will file through the biology teacher's class one after the other, year after year. Should the teacher present all these students the solution to the problem arrived at years ago, and written in the lesson plan? Or should the teacher embrace the problem anew, confront its challenges, try new ways to teach it, experiment again and again with new approaches? The simpler approach seems easier, and in a way it is, much as sitting in a dark room from morning till night is easier than getting up and walking out into the world. But if a teacher is to find and share any joy of learning as part of his or her own work, that joy will be bound up with the vivid newness of trying something new.

The very best teachers seldom rely on tried-and-true lessons. They understand the seductive power of the experiment. One high school English teacher put it this way: "My first year I had two classes right back-to-back. The same books, the same kids more or less, at 9:05 and at 10:05. The earlier class was pretty exciting. But the second class never sparked. Even the jokes that worked at nine didn't go over at ten. It took me a while to figure out the obvious. For the first class I wasn't trying to remember the lessons, or the jokes, but I was really working through new ideas with the kids. By ten I was just trying to copy myself, to reproduce what I had invented in the earlier class. It was a waste—it was all just an hour old, but it had that weight to it of something that's already growing old. I decided that I would never do that again. If I have new kids, they deserve new ideas. It's okay to bring the same questions to different classes, so long as I don't try to get the kids to come up with the same answers as the old classes did. I have to take some risks, but honestly, the time goes faster if I'm really thinking new things than if I'm trying to remember how it went last time."

Most teachers would agree, but the bureaucratic engines of school systems demand exactly the opposite: they demand lesson plans. These lesson plans revolve around learning objectives and planned outcomes. Almost without fail, more detailed lesson plans are seen as better than less detailed ones. So teachers are told to plan not only the subjects and questions they will present to their students, but also how and when these subjects and questions will be presented—at times even a blow-by-blow plan for an entire class session. This creates an environment of scripted repetition instead of genuine shared inquiry—an environment that most adults will recall from their school days. Beyond this, though, lesson planning, particularly the emphasis on outcomes, takes the process of asking questions to students and makes it to some degree dishonest by predicting and enforcing the *answers* to these questions.

Most teachers know that one of the great mysteries and joys of teaching is the fact that new groups of students have the remarkable habit of offering new—sometimes stunningly new—answers to old questions. Here's a personal example. After fifteen years of teaching Martin Luther King's "Letter from Birmingham City Jail," King's elegant defense of his presence in Birmingham, Alabama, during dramatic civil rights protests (the famous image of police dogs biting into the bodies of young African-American protesters comes from these Birmingham protests), I sat with a group of tenth-graders in an inner-city school in New England to discuss King's letter.

From jail, King explained to a group of area clergymen why he was in Birmingham:

> I am in Birmingham because injustice is here. Just as the eighth-century prophets left their little villages and carried their "thus saith the Lord" far beyond the boundaries of their hometowns; and just as the Apostle Paul left his little village of Tarsus and carried the gospel of Jesus Christ to practically every hamlet and city of the Greco-Roman world, I too am compelled to carry the gospel of freedom beyond my particular hometown. Like Paul, I must constantly respond to the Macedonian call for aid.
>
> Moreover, I am cognizant of the interrelatedness of all communities and states. I cannot sit idly by in Atlanta and not be concerned about what happens in Birmingham.

Injustice anywhere is a threat to justice everywhere. We are caught in an inescapable network of mutuality, tied in a single garment of destiny. Whatever affects one directly affects all indirectly. Never again can we afford to live with the narrow, provincial "outside agitator" idea. Anyone who lives inside the United States can never be considered an outsider anywhere in this country. You deplore the demonstrations that are presently taking place in Birmingham. But I am sorry that your statement did not express a similar concern for the conditions that brought the demonstrations into being.

I asked the tenth-graders a series of questions. Did King seem to be writing to a wider audience, beyond the local clergymen? What did he want his letter to accomplish? What was he protesting against? I received a range of engaging and vibrant answers, but largely familiar ones. Then, to my surprise, one of the students answered my last question—What was King protesting against?—in a way that changed the way I thought about the text. "He was against the government," this young man said. "He wanted less government." Less government? A libertarian, maybe even a right-wing, anti-government Martin Luther King? The student drew his point out. "Yeah, they were all saying, at least a little, that the government is the problem—the police, sheriffs, the segregation laws. Government was the problem." Then he quoted Thomas Jefferson, whom we had discussed in an earlier session: "That government governs best which governs least." It was a surprising and powerful moment. I'm not entirely convinced by the argument, but without a doubt the student was on to something important, and something I had never seriously considered, in fact never really seen in the text in years of reading, thinking about, and teaching it.

That's the power of dialogue in action. Had I focused on reaching a preestablished conclusion in my lesson on King's letter, I would never have had the chance to hear this idea. Even worse, I might have brushed it aside in order to stick to my lesson plan. But by approaching this class discussion as an experiment, an opportunity to discover something unexpected, I made it easier for a new idea to emerge. My discussion with these students was not a performance; it was a shared experiment. I didn't know what my students would find in King's letter, though I had some expectations. And yet the best outcome of that session was not the expected outcome but the surprise. Surprise is the heart of experimentation, of mixing a teacher's ideas with the uninformed but vibrant minds of students. Although much of the apparatus of modern schools discourages surprise—may even try to eliminate it from the classroom—the best teachers know its power.

In the long run, people—including teachers and students— work harder when they know they are participating in experiments. They take more interest in what they do, and they perform at higher levels. Good teachers take advantage of this. They make every class an experiment, and they make it clear to their students that new experiments are always at hand. Rather than covering a curriculum, they try to solve problems—not the problems in textbooks that are already solved and merely served to students for exercise, but real problems that have any number of possible solutions. Experiments, as the high school English teacher said, are about "making it new" for students and for teachers—keeping the life of the classroom closer to the real work of ordinary life than to the practice work of preparatory institutions. Experiments send the clear message, *This is not a rehearsal.* This is real, so pay attention.

DON'T LET THE "BIG ISSUES" TAKE OVER

In addition to these three "do's"—emphasize the individual experiences of great teachers; keep it real; and make it new—one "don't" is worth emphasizing. Don't focus on the large, abstract issues of education. Instead, if we try to solve the smaller problems, the problems that individual students and individual teachers find close at hand, the larger issues will take care of themselves. So, "How can this class be a lot better?" is a very useful question. "How can this school be a lot better?" is less useful. And dwelling on a question like "How can our schools, throughout the nation, become a lot better?" can easily do more harm than good.

A group of students I came to know in Connecticut in the mid-1990s helps to illustrate this point. A teacher in Fairfield, a suburban town populated mostly by white professional families, had been following the story of a state court case called *Sheff v. O'Neil*, which had led the state's supreme court to order the governor to submit a plan to desegregate the state's schools. Although racial segregation was not enforced by law in Connecticut, most African Americans in the state attended local schools that were mostly African American, and most white students attended mostly white schools. By the numbers, the schools were indeed segregated *de facto*. Schools in the town of Bridgeport, bordering Fairfield to the east, were largely African American; Fairfield's schools were almost entirely white, and the town of Westport, on Fairfield's western border, was if anything less integrated than Fairfield. The Fairfield teacher managed to recruit a handful of students from all three towns to gather once a week to talk about the *Sheff* case and their experiences with race in their own schools. After ten weeks the students wrote to the governor to share their recommendations as he drafted the state's desegregation plan.

The final document urged the governor to focus on the quality of classes, facilities, and pathways to college in the poorest schools before attending to the racial head count. It was an unexpected set of recommendations. It took a position at once very liberal (focus on poverty and equal resources) and quite conservative (downplay the pure racial calculus). The teacher felt proud of the students' original thinking and thought they had all gained a great deal from the ten weeks of dialogue. The students hoped for a sign that their ideas were being taken seriously by the governor, though the teacher counseled them to expect only a quiet acknowledgment—and in the end that is what they received. A letter from the governor's office thanked them for their efforts and outlined the desegregation plan the governor was about to propose.

Some of the students thought the governor had never even seen their work—the letter from his office seemed like a form letter. Others were excited by the response and felt confident that they had had an impact, if only a slight one. But all felt that the process of meeting and talking with students from other backgrounds mattered far more than the document they had sent to the governor. Their conversations, their gestures of friendship, and even their arguments formed a set of new experiences and lessons that carried far more weight in the formation of these young people's minds and hearts than any statewide desegregation plan might. The abstractions of racial politics and school policies were in the long run less interesting to them than the immediate experiences of encountering one another, learning from one another, even just hearing one another talk. The teacher's great accomplishment was in linking the big issue of race with the many small aspects of race—different expectations for college, different ways of talking, and, in fact, many similar aspirations and values. "I leave this group," one student wrote, "knowing something more than I did when I started. I hope the governor succeeds with his plan, but I think I need my own plan now too to have more time to spend with people from other places."

The idea of students taking a personal meaning and a personal challenge—the need to make "my own plan"—from the larger, more abstract issues of social policy seems like education at its best. And it can't come from the traditional study of policy issues in a classroom. It comes only from the small-scale facts of how a classroom works—who the students are, how the teacher teaches, and whether the class works toward a preconceived set of goals or encourages the vitality of real social and intellectual experiments, as the teacher from Fairfield did. Although the big issue of race was on the table for this group of students, their teacher understood that the smaller, local, human-scale aspects of race presented the best opportunities for reaching them.

2

Keeping It Real:
Education and Dialogue

Read just a little of Plato and Aristotle and you might think they are quite alike—both ancient Greeks, both philosophers, both men who thought, talked, and taught for a living. But to read them deeply is to see how fundamentally different they are. Yes, their philosophies at times shared common concerns, and sometimes they proposed similar ideas, but as writers they were worlds apart. It is almost impossible to embrace both—one so fully cancels the other out. Plato, famously, wrote in dialogues, leaning on Socrates as his main character and mouthpiece. Aristotle wrote directly to his readers, in an affirmative, direction-heavy prose. Where Socrates will ask, What is the function of drama?, Aristotle will tell us, Drama has these purposes, achieves them in these specific ways, and can be dissected into this many pieces. Teachers of classical literature tend to pick one team or the other—Aristotelians cannot, in good conscience, be Platonists. Either you fall in love with the idea of getting the world right, and telling other people to write down what the facts are, or you fall in love with the process of revealing truth through dialogue, and helping others discover the nature of the world.

Plato's habit of dialogue is of course more than habit and more than a form of exposition. It is in itself a way of understanding the world: you must talk, and then listen and think, in the company of others in order to see the world for what it is. You cannot be a philosopher as a solitary individual. You must be *in* the world to know the world. You must be among men and women, and share meals, walks, and ideas, with them, in order to know the nature of humanity. Understanding is a social activity in Plato's world.

For Aristotle, knowledge is less about society than about authority. Aristotle not only makes a literal argument for a crystal-clear hierarchy of social authority, he acts it out in his prose. He will occasionally present a survey of varying ideas on a given moral question, but then he lets the reader know which is right and which is wrong. He does not indulge in dialogue. He is a lecturer, drawing out the elements of his arguments in direct form, as though giving dictation. He has no walking and talking companions as Socrates did; instead he seems to assume an attentive audience, silently waiting for instruction. Until very recently, American schools were clearly the province of Aristotelian authority, and even in the heyday of more Platonic experiments, just about every educated American will recall far more moments of sitting, listening, and writing down than of real dialogue with teachers.

For most of American history, a good deal of schooling was informal, and until the mid-1800s more Americans were schooled in rough fashion at home than attended classrooms. Community schools outside major cities were supported in different ways— sometimes by a tax levied and collected by a local church, often by pooling the funds of students' parents, and frequently through barter (the teacher was lodged with a local family, was fed in family kitchens, and taught in a building roughly erected on a farmer's front lot). Instruction was given in the language of the community, not necessarily English (German schools were among the more common, because German immigrants were likely to establish themselves in farm communities that emphasized education but preferred to rely little on government services).

And so, as American educational institutions grew in their local fashion, immigrants from Europe borrowed the European models of instructions they knew, or at least aspired to. And that meant an Aristotelian model, altered a bit through several centuries of European styling. Students sat and practiced their grammar. They stood and recited. The teacher offered the facts, and the children (everyone hoped) drank them in. Failure to perform might mean a thrashing. And in most communities, children who did not succeed at school soon enough stopped coming, finding abundant opportunities to fill their days with farm labor from the age at which they could pick cotton, swing a scythe, or plant a seed.

Horace Mann, called far too often "the father of American education," sought to remake American schooling in the mid-nineteenth century, but he did not challenge the method of instruction that most educators and adults took for granted. Instead he worked on remaking the institutional structure of schooling. Mann championed the "common school"—a public school untethered to local churches, with a common civic purpose shared with other schools around the nation—and compulsory schooling, at least until the early teenage years. He wanted standards for teachers, rough equivalency in curriculum for all schools, and, most famously, an industrial model for American education. That meant larger schools, classing students by grade level (rather than the multi-age groupings of one-room schoolhouses), and management of the school day by the clock (and the ringing bell). In Mann's world, which soon enough became the world of the typical American school, Aristotle was still the unacknowledged master of method. Teachers taught. Students sat, wrote, memorized, and (one hoped) learned.

ALL OF HUMAN HISTORY, THROUGH THE STUDY OF COTTON

John Dewey, two generations younger than Mann, represented the first major break away from Aristotle in American education. Dewey was trained as a philosopher and certainly knew his classical Greek. But he particularly loved the philosophical work of Francis Bacon, a contemporary of Shakespeare, who coined the phrase "knowledge is power." Like Bacon, Dewey was more attracted to change and progress than to preserving received wisdom. And throughout his many books and articles, Dewey's love for the disruptive genius of children comes through. Although he was very much a man of his time—never radical in his personal habits or public persona—it is hard to imagine Dewey telling a schoolchild to sit down and be quiet. His philosophy of education was what he called "project-based learning," giving children tasks and problems to solve ("Build a house," for example), and letting their curiosity about the necessary tasks involved create the structure of their learning ("What's the best material for a roof? Why?"), with teachers ready to answer their questions. One of Dewey's most striking comments was that all of human history could be taught through the study of cotton—not because cotton is special, but simply as a random example. His point was that all of human history could be taught through the serious study of just about anything. A question like "Who grows cotton?," for example, would lead soon enough to lessons about slavery in the United States, land ownership, the nature of commodities markets, and, if we follow the chain far enough, literally everything else.

Dewey's most profound insight was less about the interconnections among all knowledge—though that is an obviously important belief for him—than about the importance of letting a student's curiosity create opportunities for memorable learning. Dewey did not wish to teach children less, or less rigorously. Rather, he wanted to tie lessons more closely to students' curiosity, and to use that curiosity as a tool for helping students learn and retain more.

The contemporary approach to foreign-language learning called "Total Physical Response" is a good illustration of Dewey's essential idea applied to one particularly apt area of learning. Using the Total Physical Response method of instruction, a language instructor might approach a new student who spoke no English at all and say, "Please stand up." The student of course would have no context for the meaning of the phrase and likely would remain seated. The teacher would then do what anyone would with a person who could not speak the language: approach the student again, raise his voice, gesture, pantomime, perhaps tug the wayward student to his feet. After a couple of rounds with this exercise, the student learns the phrase quite well. Why? Because faced with an actual person—not just a teacher at a lectern but a social agent in a social situation urging an unknown action—the student's motive to understand is vastly greater than it would be if the teacher were merely telling the class to write down the correct translation of the phrase. The Total Physical Response method extends to all kinds of physical acts and gestures ("Close the window"; "Put the book down"; and so on), each with its full social context, so that the learner has the social motive to learn. It is, in fact, one highly tailored expression of Dewey's broader approach to education—make learning real by building on the real social relationships between students and teacher.

Dewey's admonition to teachers is clear: stop pretending that the world being studied in the classroom exists apart from the classroom itself. Harness the reality and vitality of human interaction in the classroom. Use the school as a laboratory, a place of experimenting and modeling the social and practical aspects of human life, and you will accomplish more and encourage in students a greater appetite for lifelong learning. Lawrence Kohlberg, a writer and scholar of education in the 1950s and 1960s, took this idea of Dewey's a step further and looked at the classroom from the perspective of moral education. What are the effects of lessons about democracy and justice, Kohlberg asked, when given by a teacher demanding silence and obedience, occasionally beating students who do not follow the rules, in a social environment governed by a ruling class (teachers) without the consent or participation of the governed (students)? Kohlberg's message to educators was to stop pretending that questions of justice applied only outside the classroom, and that the social life of the school was somehow exempt from moral examination by students. Indeed, the moral world of the classroom taught lessons about social structure, power, and authority that no amount of lecturing about such matters could equal—or undo.

Dewey's idea of having students solve practical problems like building houses, and using the social needs that arise in that context (How does this work? How can we do this?) as motives to increase the student's appetite for learning, and Kohlberg's notion of having students examine the moral nature of their own environments (schools), may have little connection to the list of ideas that Plato revealed through the dialogues of Socrates. But they have everything in common with the humane approach to knowledge that Plato's dialogues embodied in their structure and style. As Dewey's philosophy spread throughout the United States in the 1920s and 1930s, more and more students found themselves solving real problems and having actual adventures at school. More teachers joined their students in the common work of solving practical problems, and at least a little bit of a different kind of learning found its way into American schools. As Kohlberg's ideas came into vogue in the 1970s, more teachers and students turned their analytical tools upon the social and political order of the schools themselves, and the vital ideas embodied in a hundred ancient texts took on visceral meaning for students, in their own time and place. They followed American philosopher Ralph Waldo Emerson's great dictate: "The student is to take his own life as the text, and books merely as commentary."

Why does this matter? Because these approaches to education broke down, even if only a bit, the model of the teacher lecturing and the student sitting, copying down the teacher's words, and memorizing. The moment of contact between teacher and student—a rare moment, even in "orthodox" Deweyan schools—as the teacher stands beside a student, answers a question, thinks along with the student, and offers a suggestion, is a tremendously powerful moment. It is the moment of real respect for the student as an individual. It is the moment when the generic curriculum ceases to matter and the vitality of a child's individual intelligence begins to enliven the process of learning. It is the moment when a student discovers that the very motives of life—the need to know things in order to live life moment by moment—are motives to learn and to connect with teachers, and opportunities to form social relationships grounded in respect for other people's knowledge and ideas. If we can make these exchanges between the teacher and the student—original, unrehearsed, respectful exchanges—the center of American classrooms, we can bring this moment to every student, if not throughout every school day, at least with some regularity.

What we are talking about here is dialogue, the same kind of dialogue that Socrates practices in the writings of Plato.

THE THREE PIECES OF DIALOGUE

Dialogue between a student and teacher is built of three pieces: questions, answers, and follow-up questions. The first questions a teacher asks a student—the questions that begin a dialogue—are not terribly important. Their aim is to get students reacting with some thought to an idea, an object, or a text. Then the hard work for the teacher begins: the teacher must listen well and ask for a follow-up question that begins with the student's initial observation and draws the student deeper into that observation. Most teachers don't do this. To the extent that they teach by asking questions, they tend to have answers in mind even before the question is asked. I've seen many teachers practice what I call "False Socratic Method," which involves a teacher asking a question and calling on students until one of them discovers the answer that the teacher had in mind to begin with. In this case the teacher is not really listening, and in fact the question is not really a question. It is simply an opening gambit, there to create some drama before the teacher reveals what is to be written down, memorized, and so on.

Teaching through dialogue looks easy but is not. Teachers new to dialogue often think that the trick lies in asking smart questions, and they spend a fair amount of time preparing questions for their students, in the way they might prepare a conventional lesson plan. But the great value of teaching through dialogue comes from the unexpected—from a teacher listening so well to a student that the teacher's questions help to refine and develop the original ideas that students bring to the table, rather than making structured progress toward an idea that the teacher had in mind from the start. Consider this student/teacher exchange in a third-grade class. The class has just read a story about a family that moves to a new city:

Teacher: Who is this story about?

Student: This story's about the little girl who wants to go home.

Teacher: Why does she want to go home?

Student: Because she's scared of the new place she's living. She had a place to live that she really liked, and friends and stuff, and she knew the kids who lived near her, and she knew what was around the corner and where the parks were.

Teacher: Will she ever get to think of the new place she's living as her home?

Student: Well, I don't think so. I mean, maybe she will, but first she has to feel better. She's almost like she's sick because she had to move, and that has to go by before she can feel like she's at home.

Teacher: Can you tell me more about how she feels sick?

Student: She says, "I'm lost here." And she says, "I can't breathe in this house." It's like her whole body wants to go home, so she can be better at home, and she'll just be sick where she is because she doesn't trust anyone, even though they're all the same people in her family, because they made her move.

Teacher: Is that part of her being sick, not trusting anyone?

Student: Yes.

Teacher: Will she get better?

Student: I think so. She has to spend more time there. When she learns that it's really not so different, she can probably breathe better and feel better. It's hard to move like that, but I think the story shows that her mom loves her, and when they spend more time together in the new place the girl will feel more like it's her home, but not right away. She has to be sick a little bit first, because it's hard for her to just forget all her old friends and her places. Being sick for her is like the hard part of trying to forget about her friends, or trying not to forget them.

This dialogue is quite powerful. The third-grade student generates several sophisticated ideas in response to the story. Her final remark expresses a subtle understanding of the connection between emotional and physical well-being, and her overall response to the story, and to her teacher's questions, reveals a healthy understanding of the process of transition. All the students who hear this young girl's analysis benefit from her hopeful reading of the story and her sense of the difficulty of transitions even when they turn out well.

But if you look at the teacher's questions closely, you can see that the teacher did not guide her student to these conclusions. The teacher did not have these ideas in mind, and the student did not get there through the teacher's orchestrations. Rather, the teacher listened well to the student's answers—simple, predictable, not terribly deep answers—and asked follow-up questions entirely tailored to the initial answers, in order to draw the student deeper into her own thoughts about the story. The student thought more deeply and offered ideas that were more valuable to herself, her classmates, and even her teacher, because her teacher showed her the great respect of listening well and asking skillful questions that reflected real curiosity about the girl's ideas.

The teacher's first question, "Who is this story about?," is easy enough to ask. Her second question builds on her student's specific answer to the opening question. The student said, "This story's about the little girl who wants to go home," and the teacher spotted the fact that the student answered more than the question she was asked. She not only pointed to the main character but told the teacher something beyond that character's identity. She mentioned the character's desire, her desire to go home. This added detail, the teacher knew, was a sign that the student was interested in thinking more about this extra bit of information. The teacher was looking for signs of interest like this, so her second question went directly there: "Why does she want to go home?"

The very simple question, "Can you tell me more about how she feels sick?," is the turning point in this dialogue, the moment in which the student moves away from easy answers and begins to think more deeply. When the teacher asks, "Will she get better?," the teacher is taking a risk—the student could say, simply, yes or no, and resist the deeper thought the teacher is looking for. Then the teacher might tease out more depth by following up with questions that don't allow simple yes or no responses. But a question like this—one that seems to invite a simple yes or no, but opens the door for more—allows the student to chart the course more fully, because it is so devoid of leads or prompts that might encourage the student to follow the teacher's analysis rather than the student's own. The magic of dialogue in the classroom works best when the student's ideas, not the teacher's, set the direction of the dialogue, while the teacher assures that the intellectual level of the dialogue remains high and the overall tone serious.

The point here is not that the student's ideas are by necessity better than—or even equal to—the teacher's. This approach is not about making the student the source of authority or the standard of excellence in a class. The teacher is the leading party; he or she leads the discussion toward greater depth and complexity. But as the student follows his or her own ideas, and brings deeper thought and more sustained analysis to the process of talking about an idea or a text, the student's ideas cannot help but become more sophisticated and instructive. So there are two direct benefits to this method. First, students have more patience and interest in the process of serious thinking so long as the ideas they think about are their own rather than their teacher's. Second, students' ideas are often quite original and unexpected, adding freshness and an element of intellectual excitement to the classroom. Every classroom I have ever been in could use more of both.

AN OBSTACLE TO BLIND OBEDIENCE

Some critics of dialogue-based teaching feel that making the student's ideas the center of classroom interest is not a good idea. They argue that the teacher is the adult and that intellectual originality is not necessarily a virtue, particularly when so many children aren't exposed to the core ideas of traditions that schools should be passing on to them. Stop making the kids the font of all knowledge, they say, and let them learn to respect adults more, particularly adults who have written great works and have so much to teach everyone. This is a fair criticism, particularly if one takes the preservation of tradition as the central aim of schooling. My experience has been that dialogue is not an obstacle to teaching respect, though it is an obstacle to teaching blind obedience. (If you want that, cut out the dialogue. But frankly, if obedience is the leading goal in your vision of schooling, you'll have plenty of other problems to worry about far more challenging than the effects of dialogue in the classroom.) The key to using dialogue to build a respect for tradition lies in the texts you use in the classroom. A skillful teacher can run a dialogue around the most precious texts—including religious texts—that doesn't limit the range of discussion but does help students see how their own ideas fit into the context of the traditions their teachers want them to learn about and respect.

Consider, for example, this discussion in a tenth-grade classroom. The text is these lines from Genesis:

> In the beginning God created the heaven and the earth.
> And the earth was without form, and void; and darkness was upon the face of the deep. And the Spirit of God moved upon the face of the waters.
> And God said, Let there be light: and there was light.
> And God saw the light, that it was good: and God divided the light from the darkness.

The dialogue that follows took place in a public high school, in an English class. The class was studying the Bible, not for its religious meaning but to understand it as literature. The teacher and her principal spent a great deal of time wrestling with the potential risks of teaching the Bible. Would some parents or students feel that the school was promoting religion, a clear violation of the constitutional principle of separation of church and state? Would some parents or students feel that by looking at the Bible as literature—giving it the same treatment that a novel or historical document might receive—the school was insulting the religious views of serious believers? Ultimately they decided they would try to find a middle ground, reading the text respectfully but without a religious agenda. They would read the text to make clear what it meant, and not to instruct anyone to believe it or not to believe it. They chose to use Socratic dialogue as their teaching method precisely because they felt it would allow the students to see deeply into the text without active interpretation by the teacher to promote one perspective or another. This is the dialogue they had:

> *Teacher*: What do you think is the most important line in this selection?
>
> *Student 1*: Well, I think the line about God moved on the face of the waters is the most important, because it shows that God is actually there, doing something, and not just an idea.
>
> *Teacher*: Is that an argument that you've heard before, that God is just an idea?
>
> *Student 1*: Yeah, that if you look at the Bible you see things happening that might actually not be religious or things that God is really making happen, and then we say, well, God did it, but it isn't really the story of God's work, it's just the story of the world, and God is something that we

invent. I think you could say that maybe that's true in some parts of the Bible, but here because it says that [referring to text] "the spirit of God moved upon the face of the waters," you can really see that this is a story about what God is doing, that God is the point in a way.

Teacher: What other lines are particularly important?

Student 2: "And the earth was without form."

Teacher: Why does that seem so important to you?

Student 2: Because it shows that God had to make a decision to make the world work in a certain way. First he created everything, but it was just a general kind of creation—making things exist. Then he had to give things shape, separate day from night and all that.

Teacher: Why is that important?

Student 2: Well, I think the text is saying that there's a difference here. It's Genesis—it's creation, but creation and shaping are different. It also shows that the creation was easier—God just did it. But the dividing of day and night shows God doing something different, using a different kind of power.

Teacher: How is it different?

Student 2: It's different because it's making the world have a shape, instead of just making the world. You know? It's not about the big magic of making something from nothing. It's about what that something will look like, what it'll be like to live there.

Teacher: Is that important? What it will be like to live there?

Student 1: That's a big difference. It's like when God made

the world, he was just making it for his own reasons. But
when he began making night from day, he was doing it
because he knew that he was going to put people in the
world. He was beginning to shape the experience of people,
he had that in mind, so the whole purpose of the creation of
the world begins to make more sense, because you can see
that he's doing this to make a place for people to live, for
something to happen, for a drama to take place. That's really
different from creation. That's about the drama that God is
interested in watching.

In this dialogue the students find a distinction in the opening
lines of Genesis that their teacher had never thought of, but one
that is quite interesting. The first part of the dialogue, about
whether God is an active character or "just an idea," was also intellectually challenging and ripe with possibilities. As the teacher
pressed, though, the student had little to say. So, rather than
chasing the student, the teacher opened the discussion to other
ideas, perhaps expecting to come back to the "God as an idea"
notion later.

The idea that emerges next, about the difference between the
creation of the world and the marking off of night and day, light
and dark, begins with the simple observation that "God had to
make a decision"—a significant observation that invites further
exploration. The teacher asked, "Why is that important?" and
drew the student to think about her idea, to take it further. The
teacher could as easily have asked, "What kind of decision?" a
more finely pointed question. Perhaps that would have taken the
student in a different direction, but the teacher did lead these two

students to deepen and refine their ideas. The student opens a door to a significant idea—about what the world will be like to live in—and then his fellow student takes the idea further, talking about the people who will be the ones experiencing what it is like to live in the world, and finally the idea that God is creating, and watching, a drama of sorts.

Student 1 seems more inclined to theorizing—she wanted to talk about "God as an idea," and made the intellectual leap from her fellow student's idea about the world being a place where people will live, to the notion of the world as God's dramatic playhouse. The teacher orchestrates the joint work of these two students reasonably well, though it's possible that Student 2 was left not quite grasping the ambitious ideas of Student 1. But there is time for that student-to-student education to deepen—the value of dialogue unfolds over time, well beyond the moment of conversation. Student 2 might reflect on this conversation for some time to come. Most of us process the meaning of important dialogues over days, weeks, and even years, and we need to have the confidence that if we can bring real dialogue into our classrooms, their full effects will show themselves over time. The student who walks out of the room muttering about how boring the class was might well be the one who can't get some of what went on in the class out of his mind for weeks. Or he might be the one who remembers what a teacher or fellow student had to say in that class years later, in the most unexpected moment.

The fact that this text is a foundational religious text is important in a few ways. Did the students talk about God? Yes, but not in personal religious terms or in terms of any organized religion. It might be more appropriate, in fact, to say that the students did not talk about God directly; instead they talked about *a text* about God. Should they be talking about God—or about texts about God—in a public school? They should—and if they are to be well educated, they must—talk in their schools about the texts and ideas that have shaped their history and culture. Were we to add *except for those texts and ideas about God* to this statement, we would be saying that our teachers must excise or conceal a significant piece of that history and culture. Yes, many teachers and administrators will say, religion has played an important part in our nation's public life, but it's hard and dangerous for a teacher to bring God into the classroom. Teaching through dialogue is a powerful tool for these teachers. The method helps them take the risk that the biblical text represents, because the teacher is not delivering or promoting a specific interpretation of the text. The teacher is leading a conversation about ideas, not directing his or her students to any specific conclusions at all. For the sake of helping students learn to think critically, this should be true of all texts the teacher brings to class; the fact that it helps teachers do justice to important but controversial ideas is an added bonus.

The first step to leading this dialogue well is to focus on a text. Again, in the case of the text from Genesis we're not talking about bringing God into the classroom but about bringing a text into the classroom. (Texts including the Declaration of Independence and the Pledge of Allegiance also fall into the same category of texts that talk about God.) But the text could as easily be a poem, an essay from a textbook or one written by a student, or even a painting hanging on the wall.

The second step is harder than the first: giving students time to think. That means the teacher must put up with moments of silence in class without jumping in to rephrase the question students are thinking about, or suggesting an answer to get things moving.

The next step is for students to talk and teachers to listen. Honest dialogue requires teachers to listen carefully to their students. Only by hearing what they have to say, and spotting the emerging ideas, the half-formed notions that need encouragement, can a teacher help students find their way to their own best ideas.

THE GENIUS OF UNEXPECTED TEXTS

One of the very best teachers I've seen in action was a high school English teacher in a blue-collar town near Boston who had an innate sense of how to talk with students in an honest, respectful way, without the slightest sense that he was working in a formal tradition. He was an intensely enthusiastic man, physically imposing, and made compromises every day in order to survive in a school that did not entirely welcome his knack for asking uncomfortable questions. His dream, he told me once, was to begin every day in his school with every student and teacher in the auditorium reading the newspaper. This was telling. Most of his teaching colleagues wanted to stick to their textbooks, not because those books were engaging or revealing but because they were predictable. But this teacher didn't want the predictable. He did not want to lead students to the knowledge that was already plain to see in his textbooks. He wanted to work together with his students to reach new ideas and to find the unexpected. Thus the newspapers: unexpected texts every day. News. New challenges,

72

new events, new ideas. What would a room filled with hundreds of teenagers think of the latest political scandal? What would they think of a new scientific discovery? What would they have to say about the death of a Soviet leader, or the former mayor of Boston, or a famous criminal? Anything new might be in the papers, and this teacher was almost desperate to share the flagrant reality of the new with his students, to hear them and to guide them as they faced the world's surprises. That, to me, embodied the idea of dialogue—walking beside your students as a guide and a companion in the world of ideas.

Of course, this is easier said than done, and many of the practical challenges of the classroom can seem to get in the way of good dialogue. Controlling destructive behavior and keeping students focused on the task at hand are constant challenges. But dialogue is not something that begins only when students have settled into the kind of calm, obedient state that too many people expect of them. Dialogue with students is a tool for creating a thoughtful classroom, not merely an activity that begins once thoughtfulness is imposed.

Consider, for example, this story that a Chicago teacher, Esmé Raji Codell, tells about a moment in her classroom a few weeks after she began teaching:

> I was reading them "The Hundred Dresses" by Eleanor Estes, about a Polish immigrant girl who is so poor that she wears the same dress to school every day but insists that she has a hundred dresses lined up in her closet. The girls tease her mercilessly until she moves away. Her antagonists discover that she really did have a hundred dresses . . . a

73

hundred beautiful drawings of dresses. Oh, God, it took everything not to cry when I closed the book! I especially like that the story is told from the teaser's point of view.

Well, everything was quiet at the end, but then Ashworth asked if he could whisper something in my ear. He whispered, "I have to tell the class something," and discreetly showed me that he was missing half a finger. It was a very macabre moment, but I didn't flinch.

I faced him toward the class and put my hands on his shoulders. He was trembling terribly. "Ashworth has something personal to share with you. I hope you will keep in mind 'The Hundred Dresses' when he tells you."

"I . . . I only have nine and a half fingers," he choked. "Please don't tease me about it." He held up his hands.

The class hummed, impressed, then was silent as Ashworth shifted on his feet. Finally, Billy called out, "I'll kick the ass of anyone who makes fun of you!"

"Yeah, me too!" said Kirk.

"Yeah, Ash! You just tell us if anyone from another class messes with you, we'll beat their ass up and down!"

Yeah, yeah, yeah! The class became united in the spirit of ass-kicking. Ashworth sighed and smiled at me. The power of literature!

Raji Codell does a lot with this story. She does indeed say something about the power of literature, showing how a worried boy uses the impact of a short story to create a bond with his classmates and overcome personal fears. And she reveals a lot about her style as a teacher, the kind of teacher in whose class threats and asses can find a degree of winking tolerance.

I think she also paints a wonderful picture of a classroom infused with the spirit of real dialogue with students. In her book *Educating Esmé*, Raji Codell reveals herself as a teacher who often finds powerful moments for meaningful dialogue. Part of her ability comes from a taste for risk-taking. How far can a teacher go with this chorus of threats about ass-kicking? How quickly should—or can—a teacher squelch the rough language and gangster posturing? In my experience, the best teachers react to this kind of bravado from their students the same way they might if it were coming from their friends or family. *You want to kick someone's ass? Why? Is that really the best way to deal with a problem? What's the point?* Is that a risky strategy for the teacher? Certainly. Some administrators—and some students, some parents, and some fellow teachers as well—will react more to the off-color language than to the doors those words sometimes open for learning. A teacher concerned with decorum first and foremost will punish the child for using unacceptable language (a reaction the student is probably anticipating; his language is a test of the teacher as much as it is a slip of the tongue). But a teacher always on the lookout for ways into a student's ideas might reply, simply, with the question of "Why?" A lecture on language and respect is certainly due, and must come sooner or later for this student, but the opportunity to build on this teachable moment is too precious to squander on the question of whether the student was being rude or talking about a donkey (precisely the kind of excuse the teacher can expect). So the teacher asks, Why?

How will the student reply? "Because Ash is our boy!" maybe. Or, if we're talking about a more thoughtful ass-kicker, "Because it's not right to make fun of someone like that." In both cases the teacher now has big ideas to explore. In the first case, questions like these seem ripe for the asking: What do you mean by "our boy"? Who is us? Are we any better than other people just because we're in the same class? What is it that makes us care more about Ash because he's our classmate? What kind of power did that short story have to bring us closer together as a group? In the second, questions like these: If it's wrong to make fun, is it right to kick ass? How wrong does someone have to be in their own actions before you're justified in doing something wrong—like kicking ass—in return? What if the teaser is the toughest kid in school? Does it matter whether you succeed in kicking ass, or is it enough just to try? What does it say about you as a person that you want to kick ass to protect Ash?

These are all challenging questions, and they broach subjects that most students don't do well with when presented through a typical lesson-plan approach (picture a teacher writing on the board, "Aim: to understand why we care about our fellow classmates"). But in this case the students are roused, their feelings are on vivid display to one another and themselves. They have a momentary passion that is very much driven by their own notions of right and wrong, of social belonging and social risks. This is the moment to try something more difficult intellectually, because in this moment any conversation about issues like group identity and violence—or even about "the power of literature"—is not abstract but real; not about the world in general but about the students themselves, in the very moment. And while these can be highly charged issues, in particular for students who have suffered exposure to violence in their personal lives, the context is a controlled one. The teacher points to people making fun of a classmate and then uses that concrete and controlled example as a window to a larger and potentially scarier landscape that can, in this context, be explored without necessarily leaping to the more frightening extremes. The compelling power of issues that connect to the scariest things in students' lives, like ridicule and violence, often leads teachers to avoid these subjects altogether. But these are the things that students care most about, and they certainly are things that our schools should be addressing (how could we possibly teach American history, science, or serious literature without touching on the most profoundly troubling ideas?). To avoid these risks is to avoid much of our duty to teach our children what they must learn in order to become thoughtful citizens.

In her book *Teaching Stories*, Judy Logan tells the story of an art teacher taking these kinds of risks and turning a classroom problem into a platform for serious and thoughtful dialogue with students:

One day, as Keishon [a student] is drawing a very sexy
woman in Frank's art class, Hallie [another student] walks by,
looks at the drawing, and says, "That's not art, that's sexist
trash." Frank [their teacher] puts the picture up on a bulletin
board with a sign that says "Art? or Sexist Trash?" at the top.
The class discusses which it is and why. Everyone who comes

into the room over the next days—parents, student monitors, other teachers, the principal—is drawn into the discussion. Under each heading Frank keeps a tally of how many people vote that way. It remains a running debate.

This teacher has done more than create a debate. He has sent a message to students: their ideas, their reactions to the things around them, are important. Better than a lesson in what constitutes sexism, his lesson is that differing opinions clash all the time, and that the process of thinking through ideas is as important as conclusions and firmly held opinions.

In any given school day, opportunities to explore ideas pop up many times. The teacher who tunes into those opportunities and respects his or her students enough to make their thoughts and opinions part of the curriculum does a tremendous service. That teacher's students learn that the world's complexities are not meant to be smoothed over, that debate and discussion of ideas over time lead to a richer appreciation of the world, and that attentiveness to other people's ideas will always result in unexpected lessons, reflections, and pleasures.

The common element among teachers who use dialogue well is honesty. They ask questions they are curious about—questions that are real, not questions that come from a script or seek narrow, preconceived answers. Good classroom dialogue is never a test, and never a game. It is a genuine attempt to share ideas and think together. And it is rare. In *Schools of Thought*, Rexford G. Brown describes a typical example of a teacher being less than honest in her attempts to bring dialogue into her class. Her students are reading a story about the magician Harry Houdini:

Ms. Burden asks, "What do you notice about Houdini and Boudini?" The students make some guesses, and finally one guesses, "The words sound alike," and she says, "Yes, they rhyme." She says, "Someone who does a trick is a . . ." and the students all chime in at once: "Magician." When she gives directions, she says, "Do you have any questions?" The class replies in unison, "No, Ma'am."

She moves on to teaching the concept of sequence. She asks the children, "What do you do when you get up in the morning?"

They seem confused. They look at their books for an answer.

"No," she says. "What do you do when you get up in the morning?"

A child describes his routine: he washes his face, puts on his clothes, eats his breakfast. She uses this recital to introduce the concept of putting things in order.

The greatest clue to this teacher's problems with dialogue in her class comes when she has to say "No" and clarify for her students that her question, "What do you do when you wake up in the morning?" is not a trick, not part of a script, and not a test. Instead it is a real question, something the class is not used to.

This class is apparently more used to questions like "What do you notice about 'Houdini' and 'Boudini'?" This is a funny question in two senses: it makes you laugh a little, and it is strange. It seems to have no meaning apart from an exercise in the nature of rhyme inserted into the discussion of a story about a magician, about as sensible as if a newscaster reported on floods in Mexico and then noted that "Mexico" rhymes with "Bexico." Or perhaps it is more accurate to compare this to a newscaster who reports on floods in Mexico and then notes that picante sauce from the Chiapas state is particularly tasty. After all, the picante sauce might reasonably make an appearance on the newscast in a restaurant review or feature on cooking. In a similar way, this teacher has good reason to teach about ideas and sequence, but inserting those lessons at every possible juncture, without respect for the continuity of thought that a story about Houdini would require of any sensible reader, is silly and distinctly disrespectful.

Students who assume that their job is to prepare for any possible instruction related to any word, sound, or definition included in an assigned story will perform better in this environment than those who expect a real discussion of the material at hand. Yet the winners in this game get used to a style of communication they will seldom encounter outside the classroom. Far better for teachers to lead students to expect that coherent ideas emerge from the things they read, and that learning involves careful thought as well as rapid-fire response to a teacher's questions. The students whose teacher asks questions like "What do you think?"—and then takes time to listen to the response—are lucky. The students whose teacher mostly asks questions like "What do you notice about Houdini and Boudini?" miss out on the very essence of education, that age-old exchange of ideas between teacher and student. The good teacher imparts information, asks a student to think, listens to the student's ideas, and then asks the student to think further—to take his or her initial ideas to a deeper level. This can't be done by following a lesson plan or a script. It requires respect for students and a willingness to experiment and to allow the unpredictable into the classroom, as well as a degree of self-respect that too many teachers are encouraged not to feel.

John Taylor Gatto, named New York State teacher of the year in 1991, used his newfound visibility to make the case against schools that encourage the Houdini/Boudini style in the classroom. In one essay, "The Six-Lesson Schoolteacher," Gatto outlined a number of ugly, unstated lessons that kids absorb from their teachers, including this one:

> I teach kids . . . to turn on and off like a light switch. I demand that they become totally involved in my lessons, jumping up and down in their seats with anticipation, competing vigorously with each other for my favor. But when the bell rings I insist that they drop the work at once and proceed quickly to the next work station. Nothing important is ever finished in my class, nor in any other class I know of. The lesson of bells is that no work is worth finishing, so why care too deeply about anything? Bells are the secret logic of schooltime; their argument is inexorable; bells destroy past and future, converting every interval into a sameness, as an abstract map makes every living mountain and river the same even though they are not. Bells inoculate each undertaking with indifference.

Gatto's frustration with school bells points to a larger concern: he is hungry for real dialogue with students. He wants to reach beyond the organizational needs of the school as an institution. He wants, more than anything else, to be a teacher in the traditional sense, paying all his attention to what his students think, and no attention at all to bells, to standardized exams, or to the large body of "classroom management" techniques that, as a veteran teacher, he has no doubt mastered. This is an impossible ideal in the average school, but it is an ideal worth preserving nonetheless, for in it lies the spark of hope that keeps the best teachers at work in even the worst schools.

3

Making It New:
Education as Experiment

My high school years were spent at an experimental high school, part of the New York City public school system. Named after John Dewey, my school had been founded in 1969 with multiple agendas. It was a magnet school, drawing half its students from around the borough of Brooklyn to take part in special programs. The other half of the student body came from the area neighboring the school—a public housing project. The kids from the housing project were all African American; the large majority of the kids who chose the school for its special programs were white. When I attended Dewey, the school was precisely balanced: half the students were white, half were black and Hispanic. And so John Dewey High School was a success, at least at the time, in defeating *de facto* racial segregation by artfully creating educational options that led to a kind of self-selecting desegregation, without the need for mandatory busing or race-based admissions policies.

The special programs revolved around John Dewey High School's alternative approach to learning. Dewey students were given far more choice than others in what classes they took, when they were scheduled, and, for a small number of unusually determined students, whether courses were actually taught in the classroom or conducted by independent study. The school day was longer than at other public schools, to give students more free time during the day for elective courses, clubs, and independent schoolwork. And grades at Dewey were originally pass/fail, though over time new gradations entered the system— honors, high pass, low pass, pass with condition, fail—so that eventually the grades came to look like a pretty standard structure with its own funny vocabulary.

But all the details mattered less than the atmosphere of the place. Not only did half the students attend the school by choice (and after passing an exam), but the teachers at Dewey were a self-selected group too, many of them excited to play a role in something special. Did all these teachers specifically believe in a longer school day, independent study, and pass/fail grades? By no means. But just about all of them knew that a school like this would attract kids who wanted something more from their high school years than the average school offered. Yes, many students had high grades and strong academic skills, but even among the half who chose the school, many were quite average, and more than a few were just as weak as the students of any other public high school in the city. The other half of the student body came from poverty. Some were good students, but all brought with them the challenges of low income and life in the Marlboro Houses project. Yet even these kids—many of them at least—were affected by the spirit of John Dewey High School. On average their academic work was a little better than it would have been in a typical school, and their behavior was a little better too. And, of course, they blended with the other students. In the clubs, the school newspapers, and many of the advanced classes, some of the students were from far-flung Brooklyn, and some were from the projects.

Where does the credit for this success belong? Pass/fail grades? The longer school day? The independent study courses? My sense as a student was that none of these distinct elements alone deserved the credit for the good things at the school (though some certainly deserved specific blame for the school's problems—the intentional absence of a competitive sports program, for example, seems in retrospect to have been a real loss). But more important than the specifics was the simple fact that this was a special school, an experiment. It was a school in which students got the message that they were doing something important, and that the world at large was particularly interested in what they did. Teachers competed—and at times connived—to get teaching assignments at the school. And you had to pay attention to what was going on, because that sense of business as usual, of the generic life of a high school, was simply absent at Dewey. Graduation was in June, but you *could* graduate in October (I did) or at the end of any of the school's five "cycles," miniterms that gave students the chance to switch classes every seven weeks. There was never a moment during the day when the halls were supposed to be free of students. Every period was a free period for a substantial body of students. The school day might begin at 8:05 for most, but it began an hour later for many (if they had their first period free), and a significant number of students spent one day a week away from school, working on special projects around town. It was a school where you took very little for granted, and where, at least once in a while, a student could feel a real sense of common adventure with teachers as well as with other students.

EVERY SCHOOL SHOULD HAVE
AN IDEA AT ITS CENTER

Can all schools be like John Dewey High School? Certainly not, nor would we want them to be. But every school should have an idea at its center—a notion of doing something a little differently than other schools. John Dewey High School was founded in 1969, and the reform-minded ideas at its center reflected its times. Today experimental schools are more likely to be those that emphasize a return to tradition—old-fashioned teaching styles, high standards, fewer academic "frills." Some students will do better in traditional schools, some will do better in student-centered environments, but all students benefit from being part of schools that take their missions seriously, that view themselves as centers of change and innovation, and that instill their teaching staff with a sense of mission.

In 1927 a group of Harvard Business School professors began a research study in the Western Electric Company's Hawthorne plant near Chicago. They were looking for ways to improve workplace efficiency, and they studied the effects of a range of physical

changes in the building—like brighter lights and higher tempera-
tures—as well as changes in management techniques on the shop
floor. As part of the experiment, for five years the researchers met
regularly with shop-floor employees and asked them how they felt
about their work and the various experiments going on.

Over time the researchers found something remarkable. Not
only did the changes they instituted have measurable effects on
productivity, but even in their control groups—the groups of
workers who kept on working with their old methods, in un-
changed conditions—productivity went up. Why? Because over a
sustained period of time, important-looking people asked them
how they felt about their work, and gave them the feeling that it
was very important. This effect became known as the Hawthorne
Effect. Businesses and schools too seldom take advantage of it.

Consider how a school can use the same dynamic that increased productivity in the Hawthorne plant. On the first day of
school, students are told that they will be spending the year as
part of an important experiment in education. Their school will be
a laboratory for innovation. Their opinions will be sought. Important people will want to know what they think about life at
school, about the curriculum, about the physical environment. So
much good would come from this. So why don't we do it?

At John Dewey High School the students were reminded constantly that we were part of a great experiment. What ideas were
being tested? Longer school days. More student choice in elective
courses. Less competitive grading. No competitive sports program. Now, anyone with experience in the design of experiments
would recognize that by changing so many variables at once, John
Dewey High School made it almost impossible for anyone to read

the results of the great experiment. If students left the school smarter and more capable of making their way in the world, could we credit the grading scheme? Or the long school day? Or the elective courses? Perhaps it was some special interaction of the grading and the lack of competitive sports. The bottom line is that this experiment would yield few results that another school could apply to achieve similar outcomes. From a scientific point of view, it was a terrible experiment—it was just about guaranteed to have unusable results. But from my perspective as a student there, from the perspective of most of its teachers, and from the perspective of many parents, the electricity in the air—the palpable feeling that something remarkable was happening in that building—was priceless. Dewey was, in fact, a case study in the Hawthorne effect. So many of us at the school were delighted to be part of a bold experiment that we began the typical school day predisposed to experience remarkable things at school, and that attitude helped make remarkable things happen.

A critic might say there was a fair degree of cynicism in Dewey's structure. Is it fair, for example, to call a school experimental when the goal is largely to get people more excited, without much regard for the experiment's results? One small point to illustrate: Dewey was an urban school, in an area where most school buildings stood up against their neighbors without much space for students to roam on school grounds. Dewey was lucky enough to be built on a spot of land a few acres wide on the grounds of the Marlboro Housing Project, between a city transit yard stacked with mothballed trains and an industrial swamp used years earlier to draw waste from rending plants and light manufacturing sites in the area into the tidal flows of New York harbor.

We were proud of the little campus we had, and I'd assumed that the extra space was itself part of the grand experimental design of our school. Every other high school I'd seen in Brooklyn stood shoulder to shoulder with its neighbors, with a football field tucked behind if it happened to have a standout reputation for athletics. As I grew older and traveled out of the city now and then, I was shocked to discover the wide lawns and plush landscapes of so many suburban high schools, schools that in many cases would never embrace even the slimmest of educational experiments. At Dewey the excitement of our experiment carried over even to the most mundane aspects of school life. In that environment, everything felt special. While this can be seen as a negative—we're talking about creating an exaggerated sense of importance in students, after all—what, in the long run, is wrong with allowing students to feel that all aspects of their education carry with them some great importance? Is it really possible, after all, to have students *too* excited about the broader importance of their schools?

KEEPING QUIET ABOUT THE BEST IDEAS

The New York City school system missed the opportunity to take its own experiments at John Dewey High School as seriously as it might have. It failed to move beyond the culture of experiment and study how and why things at the school worked the way they did. The idea that the experiment could be assessed and improved year by year was entirely absent. There was only the single, immensely complicated experiment that was the school itself. As for results, there they were: the school seemed to work. Little or no attention was paid to adjusting the key variables that made Dewey different from other schools beyond the small-scale tinkering that teachers employed to make things run as smoothly as possible day in and day out. As in most schools, those small changes—in this case, the quiet introduction of competitive in-school sports; de-emphasis of the seldom-used independent study kits intended as an alternative to classroom instruction—were made quietly to avoid unwanted attention from policymakers. These changes represented the best wisdom of those on the front lines of change. But they were kept quiet and were seldom discussed.

No one ever suggested that the experiments at Dewey were failing—at least not inside the school. And yet, just as I was graduating in 1981, the emphasis in the culture at large began to shift away from the school's student-centered, somewhat anti-establishment tone. Slowly the innovations at Dewey faded, a transition driven by the politics of the moment, not by a considered approach to what worked and why. But that was only fair, for the daring of Dewey's original structure was far more the product of a broad philosophy than of careful design. So much had been invested in the *ideas* of the school's innovations, but little was invested in their specific results. And school loyalists did not receive criticism of the school's programs well. That was a missed opportunity, because a loop of continuous feedback and continuous improvement is essential in applying the results of any good experiment, and gives the experiment lasting value. Continuous talk about what works and what does not, about the good ideas percolating up from frontline teachers, not only does practical good but helps to build a culture that welcomes change and values the individual.

THE POSITIVE POWER OF FAILURE

Living on the inside of an experiment is not easy. The benefits are clear: a sense of excitement; the raw pleasures of discovering new ideas; the energy that comes from being part of something new; the pride in being a pioneer. But the drawbacks can be severe. Most notable among them, of course, is the fact of failure. Experiments fail, often. If the outcome is fixed—if success is guaranteed—it's not an experiment. Indeed, failure is the *central* part of experiment. You try something, and more often than not it doesn't work. What do you get for your trouble in that case? Knowledge. You now know that one way of trying to do something does not work—and perhaps you can understand why. In this insight may lie a vision of a new possibility more precious than what you originally set out to prove. And even if a new vision does not emerge from your failure, your next attempt is still more likely to succeed, with one route to failure now known and marked to avoid. Smart scientific laboratories, the smartest public works projects, the smartest private corporations all embrace failure as part of the creative process that drives men and women toward new ideas and new levels of success. Failure can be used to kindle the spirit of experiment that makes people work a little longer, a little harder, and a little more effectively than they otherwise would.

But school systems are often unforgiving of failure. Change and experiment in schools are so hard in part because most school leaders don't grasp the value of failure. Failure is of course part of the daily life at too many schools—failure to educate, to provide a safe place for students, to reflect the best values of our communities in our schools. But so often teachers and principals—and students and parents too—keep these failures out of the spotlight. We downplay failure, and instead of using failure as an opportunity, instead of making the obvious failures in our school parts of the public conversation—indeed part of the very curriculum—we silently conspire to emphasize the few successes and ignore the instructive failures, especially the small-scale failures that should inspire small-scale experiments to reach better results.

The most obvious, most pervasive kind of failure in our schools is failure to learn. Far too many students do not learn enough to pass their classes; many more students learn enough to pass, but fail to learn more. This is a vast category of failure, and one we generally pass over with little concern. The student who earns a B or a C—or even an A—without mastering all that he or she could have mastered, has failed, though it may be wiser to think of these students as the measure of their schools' failure. This failure is hardly life-altering for most of these students, but it is unnecessary and less difficult to remedy than most imagine. The remedy lies in direct contact between a teacher and student. To the teacher with thirty students in a classroom, engagement with an individual student's work is difficult. What modest incentive there is for one-on-one contact usually concentrates on representative written work and exams. Precious little time is spent in direct conversation with students. The only way for the teachers to review every bit of students' written work is to assign little of it.

Imagine, though, a school where every student spends hours every day in one-on-one discussion with teachers, where written work is extensive and always reviewed by one teacher with the student at his or her side. This sounds like an unaffordable ideal, but a former public school superintendent in Phoenix, Arizona, named David Curd now runs three public high schools that manage to pull it off, at a cost of roughly $5,000 per year per student. He began with a simple observation about failure. "There was just no question," he said, "that kids were failing who didn't have to fail, that teachers who wanted to help kids learn often just weren't, and that there were lots and lots of kids who were dropping out of school who didn't need to drop out. At the same time, you had plenty of kids who were staying in school but not learning what they could learn because nobody was sitting down with them asking questions as general as 'What did you think about the book you just read?' or as specific as 'How do you do long division?' So we said that we would try to do that, that we could find a way to make a new school where we admitted what wasn't happening, what kids weren't learning, and we'd find a way to fix it.

"The biggest barrier, we thought, would be money. But we were wrong—money was not a problem. If you think like a school system, you figure all the costs of running a school the usual way, and you multiply that by however many more teachers you want in order to have every student sitting with one teacher and getting individual attention. We didn't do that. The real smart thing we did was first to get better use of the big expensive things at a school, like the school building. And we noticed what a lot of kids who drop out want. Most important to them is a more flexible schedule, so they can work or watch their own kids or take care of a sick mother. This actually helps the financial picture a lot. We have each building serving lots of kids, because our flexible schedule lets more kids be enrolled in school, but fewer are in the building at any one time. That means you need a much smaller school building—or if you want to do what we do across a whole big district, a lot fewer schools."

The flexible schedule at Curd's schools, operating under the umbrella of the Institute for Humanities and Sciences, runs for twelve hours a day, five days a week. School opens at 7 a.m. and stays open till 7 p.m. The full range of instruction is offered all day. Students are required to be in school working with teachers at least twenty hours a week (the same amount of instructional time that students receive in traditional public schools in Phoenix). But at the Institute for Humanities and Sciences, instruction does not mean classes. The large majority of instruction is delivered one-on-one, and students decide for themselves which twenty hours in a given week they wish to be in school.

The curriculum is highly structured, and students carry with them a simple record of what they are doing in each subject. They present that record to the teacher they choose to work with on a given subject for a given day. The teacher can see at a glance what the student needs to do for the next lesson in the sequence of coursework, and gets to work guiding the student through more challenging material and engaging the student in dialogue, drawing out the student's understanding of the work at hand. Students are not allowed to progress to their next lessons until their teachers feel confident they have learned at least 90 percent of the current material. Working one-on-one with students gives teachers that opportunity to know exactly how each student is doing. The failure to learn, even among the most successful students in many classroom-based schools, fades considerably.

Criticism of the Institute for Humanities and Sciences takes many forms. One common concern is that students lose the value of socializing that comes from the traditional classroom experience. Another is that without a traditional sports program, students lose out. The Institute tries to face these challenges through an intensive out-of-school program that groups students together every day to sail, fish, and explore other sports, takes them to Mexico for intensive marine biology study, and brings them to a range of other fieldwork sites.

Certainly the program is not for every student (about 20 percent of the students who enroll in the Institute choose to return to traditional schools), but the Institute stands as a remarkable example of honest assessment and response to one of the fundamental failures of so many schools—the failure to help every student learn as much assigned coursework as he or she can. It is a distinct alternative to the mass-production model of schooling that sets passing as 65 percent of success.

SCHOOL VIOLENCE AND THE ILLUSION OF SOLUTIONS

Another kind of fundamental failure that we often ignore in schools is the failure to keep students safe. Most educators who work with violent students agree that some of the best ways to prevent serious school violence are those that would make education in general better: more contact between individual teachers and students; more opportunities for students to speak with teachers beyond scripted question-and-answer exchanges; and more adults ready to take students seriously. Taking a threat of violence seriously is not that different from taking a student's ideas seriously—both are a function of respect.

Schools tend to resist doing these things for a number of reasons. Creating more one-on-one relationships between teachers and students represents a fundamental change in the typical school's approach to education, and change is hard. Thoughtful interaction between individual teachers and students is quite different from the structured and scripted models of classroom excellence that most school systems celebrate, and getting beyond this deeply rooted emphasis on lesson planning is a great challenge. Opening the door to the unpredictable nature of genuine dialogue is a great threat to many teachers and administrators because predictability is one of the cardinal virtues in the typical American school. All these elements of standard American education today—an emphasis on the group over the individual; planned and controlled lessons, an emphasis on the predictable—are precisely what Horace Mann fought to achieve in the nineteenth century. Faced with a nation of one-room schoolhouses, barely literate teachers paid at poverty wages, and instruction in public schools that ranged from the overtly religious to the clearly erroneous, he imposed order and the beginnings of national quality standards in education. The question of school safety seldom arose during Mann's lifetime, in part because personal expectations of safety were so different in the nineteenth century, but also because schooling was considered a privilege. Violent students were easily expelled, along with students who performed poorly and others who simply were not wanted. One hundred and fifty years later, our schools grapple with a mandate to *educate* the potentially violent student rather than banish him.

In this new world, the central question about safety that most schools ask today is, "How can we prevent the intensely violent incidents that make the television news?" Too few schools focus on the low-level kinds of violence that lay the groundwork for greater disasters. Almost none draw the connection between the seemingly random bad luck of enrolling violent students and the unmet need for teachers to spend more time in genuine dialogue with students to learn what they're thinking. This is a missed opportunity of enormous proportions.

Consider school violence from the top down and you find a small number of terrible prospects for violence that can be fought with school-wide safety initiatives, metal detectors, and similar steps. The problem of school violence from this perspective takes the form of bad outcomes—fights, injured students, a threatening climate in the hallways, and bad press, particularly among parents. Anti-violence policies can address these problems in practical ways, including vigilant patrolling of the hallways, checks for weapons, and active outreach programs to help students feel comfortable in reporting rumors of violence. But from the bottom up, things look different. Violence is less a matter of violent outcomes, more a matter of a feeling of fear in the air. Relatively few students are actually harmed physically in rough schools, but many—perhaps all—are touched by fear and anxiety, by the feeling that the adults in the school cannot control and often don't really know the worst that might happen at any moment.

Picture a school poised to address violence. The leadership might make any number of changes, but if those changes are seen as solutions rather than as experiments—if those changes are defended, buttressed, and fought for (because they are seen as solutions), rather than constantly evaluated and tinkered with (because they are seen as experiments)—much is lost.

An emphasis on dialogue in the classroom can help. Schools that create many opportunities each day for teachers and students to exchange ideas are not necessarily safer places. But the very idea that teachers take a student's ideas seriously—that teachers are concerned not only with how a student acts but with how he or she sees the world—contributes mightily to the kind of school in which secrets are rare and students' characters are better understood. These are two extremely important factors in preventing violence. Making schools less violent, after all, is part of the larger project of changing the way students communicate and express themselves toward one another. If we value thoughtful communication, honest expression, and long-term thinking over the impulsive, the self-serving, and the shortsighted, teachers should express the same values as they work with their students, and should respond to them as thinking individuals in the classroom.

One school in New England that I visited for a year is typical of a well-intentioned institution that has failed to make its fight against school violence as effective as it could be. After several years of frightening violence in and around the school, a new principal appeared on the scene with a range of reform plans, including a priority on school safety. He hired half a dozen security officers, called "monitors." When classes changed, the monitors would make sure that all students were inside the classrooms for their next courses within a few minutes. By the time the second bell rang, letting everyone know that the next class was officially under way, the monitors were yelling at students struggling in the halls, moving in on the slowest of the laggards and hanging over them until they entered their next classes. The monitors used every bit of leverage they could, including intimidating students socially and physically. Under this new regime, the halls were clear on time. Violence overall inside the school went down—a result of a number of other new policies, including a good deal more teacher presence in the hallways. The problem of outcomes was solved, at least to a degree, because the school hallways became safer (though a good deal of violence remained in the surrounding area, and students were often involved in fights and assaults near school).

But the larger issue was not resolved. A trade-off had taken place: instead of being intimidated (and assaulted) by other students up to no good, now the average student was intimidated by the monitors. Most would probably agree that the trade-off represented a kind of progress. The net result was a safer school. But the school's leaders did not solve the broader problem because they never openly addressed the failure in terms of the average student's experience in the school. They reduced the number of violent incidents—a very good thing—but they never addressed the school's failure to create a culture in which intimidation and force took a backseat to respect and reason. It was a missed opportunity.

THE VALUES OF OUR COMMUNITIES

A third kind of failure that we seldom discuss is the failure to have our schools reflect the best values of our communities. This goes well beyond issues of violence. Consider, for example, this story that Judy Logan tells in *Teaching Stories*:

> One day Lia looks depressed. She is a straight-A student. "What's wrong?" I ask.
>
> "I got something wrong on my science test," she says.
>
> "What?" I ask.
>
> "Well, the test was on class rules. It was a fill-in test. The question was 'The legs of your chair should be on the yellow blank,' and I wrote *line*."
>
> "What was the correct answer?" I ask.
>
> "It should have been 'The legs of your chair should be on the yellow *mark*.'" (This teacher has painted yellow lines— sorry, marks—on his floor so the students' desks will be lined up in neat rows.)

Now, this science teacher might well be prone to pettiness in every aspect of his life, but there is something about life in the typical American school that leads too many teachers to become more concerned with lines on the floor than with the ideas of science or the intellectual pleasures of whatever subject they teach. This story reveals a type of behavior that bureaucracies encourage with their emphasis on rules and procedures. In a way this is a sad epitaph for a teacher who in all likelihood would be ashamed of his own behavior if he were to view it at some distance. But too many times, in too many schools, we value process over substance, and obedience over the spirit of learning. While there are perfectly good excuses for doing this, there is never justification. The best values in our communities, and in ourselves, belong in our classrooms.

So long as school systems emphasize whole-school and whole-district planning—even planning for great-sounding reforms—the systems and structures of our schools will impose on teachers the need to conform. Teachers will in turn impose the same kind of conformity, too often, on too many students, as Judy Logan's story demonstrates. Teaching and learning, after all, are highly personal acts. The student who fails her science test because she cannot remember the right word for the imaginary mark upon which to set her chair—but who may well have learned lessons in biology or astronomy brilliantly—is essentially being punished for trivial aspects of the *way* she learned (in this case, with her chair in a different place, or without the mandated vocabulary for class rules) when it is the learning itself that should be cherished.

THE WISDOM OF LOOKING HARD
FOR FAILURE

These examples of failure are, in some ways, subtle. A school leader who has lowered the rate of violent incidents in school is unlikely to notice the broader failure to create an environment that *feels* safe to students. That same leader is likely to end a day in the trenches by feeling that his real priority is recruiting desperately needed teachers or short-circuiting a crisis looming among graduating seniors who are failing their classes, rather than the failure of the community's best values to find their way into his classrooms. Problems like community values are just too far removed from the urgency of daily school life to seem important enough to address. And that is why teachers, students, parents, and administrators must make failure a regular and comfortable topic of discussion. Only by looking hard for these kinds of failures will we find them, and only then can we work to fix them, hopefully by making dialogue a central feature of the classroom.

But it's not easy to make this happen. Most parents, students, and even teachers themselves have the habit of exacting a high price in the face of failure. They want no part of it. They hate failure enough to reject the whole idea of experimenting with education (as if education could exist without experiment). Don't experiment on *my* kid, or with *my* last year of high school, or in *my* classroom, many will say. They worry over the prospect of failure, partly (and rightly) because they may not be around long enough to benefit from the ultimate success it may lead to, but also because they haven't been exposed to the thrill of the hunt that a good experiment creates. For in the long run, it is not the ultimate success of an experiment that justifies it, but the value of being part of an earnest effort to discover something new.

"The best thing about my school," says a student at a charter school in Chicago, "is that we're all working together to build something. I know that next year and the year after that, when I'm gone, there's things that I did this year that will still be here, things about what the classes are, how the building looks, how other students are going to do their work, that are part of what I got to do. It's great to be the first ones at a school like this. You really feel like you're doing something special. My goal here is to do things a little differently. Everything you do here is a decision. You have to think about everything, because there's no old way to do things. You invent everything, you make a choice all the time."

Consider the example of a school that experiments with pass/fail grades. In the early 1970s this was not an uncommon kind of experiment in American high schools, though today's competitive climate in schools has led most of those high schools back to the standard scale of A to F. In too many cases these schools were experimenting with grades in the way that John Dewey High School did. They changed policy and waited to see what happened next. The important question many of these schools never answered was, How will we know when we succeed? By not making clear the goals of the experiment, any experimenting school runs the risk of setting out to be innovative but instead becoming purely reactive to the temper of the times. In a conservative moment the experiment might become some variation of "back to basics." In a more adventurous moment the experiment might fly under the banner of freedom and independence for students. But thoughtful support for experimenting in and with schools can get students and teachers beyond the fad reforms of the moment and onto solid and exciting ground.

In this hypothetical example of a school experimenting with pass/fail grades, one temptation at the outset will be to announce soft measures of success like "smarter, more engaged students." But with harder measures like higher grades, or more hours spent on extra-curricular activities on school grounds, the leaders of the experiment can get a good read on their results over time and actually apply the lessons learned. So if the experiment is to try pass/fail grades, let's assume that one of the goals of the experiment is to lessen student anxiety and encourage students to stretch their abilities and try subjects that are outside their comfort zones, without having to worry about hurting their grade point averages. The leaders of the school might measure the number of students enrolling in advanced math and science courses at the end of two years of the experiment.

Assume a poor outcome to this experiment. After two years the school discovers that very little has been accomplished—few new students are taking the more challenging and typically "scary" courses. So the experiment has not been a success. But some knowledge has been gained. There's the obvious knowledge: this specific strategy did not work. The school isn't likely to try it again, and that's one possible failure it can avoid in the future. Better, though, is the knowledge this bit of experience can yield when interpreted in the real-life context of the school, with all the personalities, social dynamics, and other "soft" factors thrown into the equation. Pass/fail grading didn't work. Why? Perhaps in this community a competitive spirit is important to motivating students. If this is true—and if the experiment helped to make this clear—the school has learned that competition is an important factor. Not only will new innovations hew more toward the idea of productive competition, but teachers can engage the very idea of competition as part of the curriculum. Having students discuss and evaluate the experiment that failed is a great tool to raise the level of student energy and commitment. In this case it also helps students better understand the nature of competition, and their own natures.

Thus three levels of value come from this hypothetical experiment, even though it failed. First, this approach gets crossed off the list of methods competing for time and attention. Second, a whole category of similar approaches now might seem worth avoiding, in this case, methods that don't take advantage of the school's competitive spirit. (This potential shift to entirely new kinds of methods to improve students' comfort with harder courses could be dramatic. It represents a new strategy based on actual experience instead of well-intentioned guesswork.) Finally, by involving students in the process and carefully considering the experimental part of the students' schoolwork, students see immediate connections between their studies and the rest of their lives.

As if all these benefits were not enough, once in a while *experiments actually work.*

4

Recruiting and Retaining
the Right Teachers

One moment in the struggle to improve our schools represents the ultimate in bottom-up reform. It is the moment when we decide whom to hire as teachers. It will always be much easier to encourage talented, dedicated people to improve markedly than it will be to coax people without these qualities to change even a little. So we must exploit the leverage we have at the moment of hiring and select only the very best candidates.

Several recent studies have identified the characteristics of teachers who help students perform better: expertise in an academic subject other than education, high college grades overall, and high scores on college entrance exams like the SATs. Look at the classes with teachers who have these qualities, and, on average, students in those classes will be getting better grades and testing at higher levels than students of the same background whose teachers were education majors rather than, say, history or biology majors, whose teachers had lower grade point averages in college, or whose teachers had lower SAT scores.

Linda Darling-Hammond, a professor at Stanford University, published in January 2000 perhaps the most striking study of teacher quality in relation to student performance. Using data from every state in the Union, Darling-Hammond concluded that "teacher quality variables appear to be more strongly related to student achievement than class sizes, overall spending levels, teacher salaries (at least when unadjusted for cost of living differentials), or such factors as the statewide proportion of staff who are teachers." The professor's language underemphasizes the remarkable results of her study. Her work answers the question of whether having a smaller class, or a teacher who took more subject-specific courses and got higher grades, results in students doing better. The answer is that the smarter teacher helps more than the smaller classes. Another question the study answers: What is more important, growing up in a financially well-off home, or going to a school where the teachers scored higher on their own exams? Again, the study showed that smarter teachers helped more. These findings go against the presumptions of many education professionals, and they reveal the tremendous importance of the leverage we have when we hire teachers.

THE AVERAGE TEACHER

Unfortunately the average American teacher is not at the top of the class—literally. The College Board's Graduate Record Exam is a test that most students take as part of the admissions process

108

for graduate studies—similar to the SAT for undergraduate studies. How do educators fare on that test, in comparison with seven other professional categories that the College Board tracks? Last.

And on the SAT, students identifying themselves as future education majors score, on average, 964—below the overall average of 1016, and still lower than the average test-takers in suburban schools at 1050.

Are there fantastic teachers who had low grades, majored in education, or recorded very low SAT scores? Without a doubt. Should we exclude them from the teacher corps? Not at all. But when these people are hired as teachers, we should watch very closely to see whether student performance follows the statistically likely course—and declines or remains low—or whether the teacher in question can buck the odds and come out a winner.

We should, of course, hire teachers who are most likely to succeed, which generally means those with superior academic backgrounds, the best communications ability, and the greatest commitment to kids and teaching. But when an individual does not hit all three categories—and many won't—we must save our sense of kindness for our children and resist the temptation to be kind to less-talented teachers at the expense of the students they would serve poorly. In the end, the only way to ensure that our teachers are extraordinary educators is to find ways to steer the ordinary ones into other jobs.

The question here is simple: do we want teaching to be an elite profession? The idea of elites—that some people are better at their jobs than others, and that an informed and diligent observer can tell the difference—will raise the hackles of many people. They will say that, first of all, any judgment of one professional over another is fraught with subjectivity and cannot be completely fair. And is this what we want to teach our students—that some people are better than others? Aren't there better social values we can take to the head of the class for our students to learn from? These are valid concerns, but a bit of triage is in order. We can put the idea of equity and fairness to teachers ahead of a better education for the students, or we can begin with the absolute commitment that students come first, and that we must ensure the best education for students and then work to achieve fairness and equity for everyone else.

The world already knows that teaching in America today is not an elite profession. Consider this snippet from a recent *Wall Street Journal* article:

> In America, teachers have nearly always been shortchanged relative to other professionals. Now, with the nation in its longest economic expansion on record and the New Economy creating new levels of wealth and new class divisions, the ignominy is only worsening, financially and in other ways. The pay stinks. Parents are often pushy. And social status is slipping.
>
> "Among well-educated and wealthy parents, there is a pervasive, unspoken condescension bordering on contempt toward the less-well-educated and less-wealthy teachers who work at their schools," says Tom Sobol, former school superintendent in affluent Scarsdale, N.Y., and now a professor at Columbia University's Teachers College.

The question we should take up, then, is what we can do about this.

Recruiting and Retaining the Right Teachers

The first answer is apprenticeship. If we are to transform teaching into an elite profession, a period of apprenticeship is vital—and that means real apprenticeship, not merely lower pay for the same job that experienced teachers have (the regime that most school districts currently enforce). We need to offer new teachers a period of a few years in which they learn a great deal about how schools work by actually being in the classroom, and in which the school community learns a great deal about the individuals who want to be teachers. Key to the notion of apprenticeship is a dual evaluation: the new professional learns about the profession, and the key constituencies of the profession learn about the apprentice. The notion that any and every apprentice should proceed from the apprenticeship to the profession makes no sense. It flies in the face of the obvious fact that some people are better at a given job than others, and it prevents us from reacting reasonably to what we learn about the people who apprentice as teachers.

If we want good schools populated by talented teachers, at the end of the apprenticeship period—and this is the hard part—about half the new teachers should be congratulated on their good work and sent on their way to different careers. The other half—the best-performing half—should be embraced as new journeymen teachers ready to begin the second chapters of their careers. This might seem wasteful, even cruel, but consider this: in many school districts in the United States, in the first three years of teaching experience, well over half of all new teachers quit on their own. In far too many cases they quit not because the work is too hard or because they can't live up to high standards, but because these young people discover that the culture of teaching is too often one of mediocrity, filled with folks who aren't the brightest, aren't expected to work at very high intellectual levels, and don't have the pride that excellence brings. Many of the very best new teachers move to other fields that self-select an elite, so they help maintain the cycle of mediocrity among teachers. In other words, the half that quits is the wrong half—they're the ones we should most want to keep.

Many people who are concerned with attracting the right people to teaching careers point to the relatively low pay in the profession as one of the most important challenges we must overcome. Teachers' salaries certainly are relatively low, and the financial sacrifice becomes greater over the years. Young teachers make less than their peers in other professions, but not terribly much less. Veteran teachers, whose nonteaching peers have spent a couple of decades working their way up the pay scales in their professions, make dramatically less. The numbers tell the story: starting pay for the average teacher in the United States is at the very bottom of what professionals in any field make. In the boom decade of the nineties, teachers' salaries rose, on average, 10 percent nationally, compared to an average 42 percent increase for business administration professionals and 36 percent for computer professionals. In an era in which well-educated people in our country have become yet more prosperous, the gulf between what teachers earn and what their friends with similar education earn in other fields has only widened. The average teacher—not a newly minted college graduate but the average across the board— earns $32,600 in Texas. In Massachusetts, $43,800. In California, $43,500. Florida teachers earn, on average, $33,900. Working as a teacher is challenging; supporting a family on these salaries is extremely difficult, particularly when higher salaries are readily available in other professions.

MONEY IS NOT THE MAIN MOTIVATOR

Most professionals do not have to look far to find a number of former teachers now working in other jobs. Many of them will mention money as one of the reasons they left teaching, but few will point to it as the principal reason, and this is an important fact. Money is more likely to keep people from considering teaching in the first place, but "softer" issues—issues of respect, institutional support, and personal professional standards—are the ones that cut deeper for many of the most promising teachers, and they are harder to address than financial issues.

One young woman from Texas describes her decision to leave teaching in dramatically clear terms: "I wanted to teach younger kids, and I got exactly what I wanted. Everyone I knew warned me about teaching in Dallas, about the poor kids, the violent kids, the kids who couldn't learn. They were right in a few cases, but wrong overall. These kids were fantastic. Some were stinkers, but even they had a spark of youth that they couldn't hide, and they did try to hide it, oh yes they did. But no one told me about the other teachers.

"I was working in a school that teachers would transfer out of once they had the seniority to get assigned elsewhere, mostly to safer neighborhoods, where they thought the kids would be different. I doubt the kids were different—we're talking about nine-and ten-year-olds here, and I can tell you from experience that these children might look different, dress different, and even act a little different in this neighborhood or that neighborhood, but these children are not different. They are the same innocent, crazy, frustrating, brilliant little things anywhere you go if you look at them long enough. But the teachers, boy they were different. They were different from me, from my education professors, from my friends, from my family. They didn't want to work. They didn't want to teach. They were just punching the clock, that simple. And I hated that. They made me angry. I had kids I'd send up to the next grade and I'd feel like I was sending them to jail. I just could not stand that another year. I had the chance to stay and in two more years I could have bid to go to a nicer school, which was tempting because I was pretty sure I would find teachers there I could become friends with, but I was just too turned off to the whole system at that point. But I do miss those kids."

This teacher was turned away from a career in education because she had colleagues she thought were destructive. She wasn't proud to work among them, they didn't help her become a better teacher, and she had no hope for positive change in her school. Her situation might well have been worse than the average American school provides, but the dissatisfaction that led her to leave teaching in Dallas is far too present in just about every school system in the country.

What would this Texas teacher's working life have been like if all her teaching colleagues had earned their places in the classroom by demonstrating more ability than the average applicant for the job of teacher? Would she be as likely to see her colleagues as clock-punchers? I doubt it. If young professionals setting out on their careers knew that teachers were vetted to high standards, many of the most talented, who now go to other professions, would be teaching beside this woman in Texas, enriching her school's professional environment, helping fulfill our culture's promise to the students who show up there every morning.

CROSSING A THRESHOLD

New teachers must come to know that there is an early-career, merit-based threshold to cross, similar to what doctors, lawyers, and many business professionals face in their first few years of professional work. If we can make this a reality, the most talented and most effective among them will be able to earn their place in a truly elite, dedicated corps of teachers. We will keep the very best of the new teacher recruits, and we will attract large numbers of people in other professions who today don't sign on to become teachers because they believe that American schools haven't fostered a culture of achievement and haven't been able to make the profession of teacher as respected or respectable as many other professions. That's an unfortunate situation, but not liking the situation should not blind us to it. Far more than higher salaries, a culture of elite professionalism will attract and retain precisely the people who we know are the better teachers—people with higher grades, the best communications skills, and the greatest knowledge of the subjects they'll be teaching. Money certainly matters, but professional culture matters more, and will be a greater challenge to make right.

In many school systems today, new teachers are, officially, on some kind of probation for a period, often three years. But these probationary periods in fact do not relate to job performance. So long as performance is not outright criminal or grossly harmful to children, new teachers in these districts will keep their jobs. The money in school budgets is the key to launching or limiting their careers. In the event of a budget cutback, the probationary teachers are the ones whose ranks are trimmed, because they are generally not fully covered by unions and are therefore easier to let go. So long as we do not screen new teachers based on excellence—not based on mere competence or basic skill levels, but based on a demonstration that each individual is better at teaching than most who try—we will never be able to create and reinforce the kind of elite professional culture among our teachers that they deserve, and, more important, that our students deserve.

We must do more than demand excellence on paper. Today a remarkably large percentage of school districts have standards for the hiring of new teachers, and for the movement up from probationary status into the mainline teaching corps, that are fantastically strong—but only on paper. As Lynn Olson recently wrote in *Education Week*, official "standards mean nothing if schools can wiggle around them by hiring people who don't meet the requirements whenever there's a spot to fill. As a result, millions of students sit down each day before teachers who don't have what their states consider the most basic requirements for being there. That common practice—known by such euphemisms as 'emergency' licensure, 'incidental teaching,' or 'misassignment approval'—is used to fill classrooms when teachers in a particular subject can't be found, or when teacher candidates haven't passed a test or finished their coursework."

Olson goes on to cite the National Commission on Teaching and America's Future, which reports that 12 percent of new teachers are hired without any teaching license at all, and another

15 percent are hired with emergency, temporary, or incidental licenses. The United Federation of Teachers, the second largest teachers' union in the United States, reports that in New York City in the 2000–2001 school year, 60 percent of new teachers were uncertified.

The numbers do not inspire confidence in our school systems' ability to enforce their standards. This is not a portrait of an elite culture. This is a portrait of a bureaucratic culture in which the getting or filling of the job becomes more important than teaching students as best we can. Improving the quality of the teaching corps has a dramatic effect that no other reform can match: it makes schools much better for poor students as well as for the middle class. Giving the poorest, and the poorest-performing, students better teachers does them more good than any other change we can make in their schooling, bar none. To focus on the elite among new teaching recruits is the radically democratic way to give our society's very best resources to our poorest and neediest children. That simple fact should trump any concerns about the ill effects of meritocracy among job applicants.

A FAILURE OF LEADERSHIP AND POLICY

What we are looking at today is not a failure of our existing teaching corps. Rather, we are facing a failure of policy and leadership in how our schools are run. To examine our national system of education, and to identify opportunities to improve it, is not to denigrate the teacher corps. To point to the character of the professional environment for teachers—to say that it is not an environment that encourages and reinforces an elite—may sound like an attack on teachers, or an insinuation that elite individuals, even brilliant individuals, do not wish to become teachers. That would be a terrible mistake. I've personally been taught in public schools by some of the most brilliant men and women I have ever met. I've taught alongside, and been a professional observer of, public school teachers whom I would match against any of the people I taught with at Harvard and Columbia. But we must be honest enough in our evaluation of the current state of our schools to note that these outstanding people—and there are tens, perhaps hundreds of thousands of them in our public schools today—go against the grain of the professional culture of our schools. They are not only the best, they are in a way the dissidents, the people who stand out, who attract criticism as well as praise for being remarkable educators, and they resist a strong pull toward mediocrity in the professional culture of too many schools.

A few years ago I wrote a book about a school in Massachusetts that painted a "warts and all" picture of an urban high school. It had some fabulous teachers, and some pretty poor ones. It was a typical school in many ways, with the full range of problems and opportunities. One teacher in particular stood out—a "natural" teacher, a man who lived for the ideas his students brought into school with them every day. He stood out as a character in the book, as he did in the school itself, as an unusual and effective educator. A local weekly newspaper wrote a story about the book when it was published, taking a largely defensive tone, seeing the book as the work of an outsider, a college professor without fair standing to criticize the school. The paper's photographer took a photo of this extraordinary teacher and used it prominently in the article. The next day, in the teachers' bathroom, some of his colleagues had hung the photo, circled some of the words of praise from the book that were repeated in the photo caption, and written curses across the photo. This was an ugly illustration of something very wrong in the professional culture among educators in one particular school, and it is an extreme case. But it shows how important the professional culture can be in every teacher's life, and it reveals how destructive that culture can be at its worst.

The single most significant step we can take toward creating more of an elite professional culture for our teachers is to change the expectations of new teachers. Today most teachers who get their necessary teaching credentials and licenses expect that once they've found teaching jobs, those jobs are essentially theirs to lose. So long as they don't fail in the grossest and most obvious ways, and so long as their schools have the money to keep their positions funded, they'll be able to keep their positions by putting in a fair day's effort for each day's pay. That's a pleasant work environment, but it does not foster the best possible teachers for our children.

In elite professions, entry-level employees expect that the senior positions in their fields are theirs to *earn*, not theirs to lose. Big-city law firms tend to have an "up or out" track—young lawyers are expected to demonstrate that they are outstanding, among the very best in their peer group, or eventually they will be asked to leave. That expectation drives many excellent young lawyers out of good firms. Knowing the tough advancement policies, they often accept other professional opportunities without ever facing the prospect of dismissal. Because they are already part of an elite organization with well-known standards, other employers seek them out. They actually benefit from the high standards, even if they don't make the cut. Just being part of the team enhances their career options.

Academia is similar. A young science professor knows she has to do notable work in order to be offered tenure at her university, and that many, perhaps most, of her peer group won't make the cut. They'll go off to other academic positions, perhaps less prestigious ones, or to administrative positions, or to the private sector. These are very tough professional expectations. They leave a lot of young professionals frustrated. But they also create a senior professional rank of unparalleled excellence. Those who fill the law partnerships at the larger firms, and those professors at elite institutions who achieve senior, tenured professorships, are without a doubt an elite group, and the process helps to perpetuate a level of excellence and high professional standards.

These standards may not be the best ones—perhaps teaching should be more strongly emphasized in the academic science departments; perhaps mentoring and long-term decency should be more the point among law partners. But seeing that these standards have an impact, whatever the specific standards are, is the hard part. The standards are there not so much to reward the winners at the top of the professional ladder as to shape the expectations of younger professionals and ensure their firm dedication to excellence. Yes, this is ungenerous and in many ways unfair to the young professionals, but it ensures that the quality of their work is a higher priority than their personal experience. The work of educators is to educate young people. So long as we have the courage to make the very best experience for those young people our highest goal, we must attend to fairness for teachers only after we have attended to excellence for our students. And today we have yet to do that.

A CASE STUDY

Consider the college student planning to become a teacher. And consider not just any student but the kind of student we most want to be teaching our children—someone who is bright, warm, disciplined, and interested in other people's ideas, someone curious about the world and capable of doing difficult things well.

At the age of twenty-one or so, he (let's use a man in this example) is finishing college, heading toward a degree in English, biology, history, or another subject. Most likely he is not taking a degree in education (the students with the strongest academic backgrounds generally don't). In his senior year he is probably working as a student teacher for at least part of the year, going off in the mornings to a school where the students call him "Mister." He takes a coffee break in the teachers' lounge now and then, a junior colleague of teachers who are young and old. His friends who are not planning to become teachers are studying, heading off for the occasional job interview, and spending a great deal of time as college students do—enjoying their independence, hanging out, reading interesting books, thinking about the future. In this local culture the student teacher is a standout. He's in the real world, seen by many as a full adult citizen, clearly bearing serious responsibility for the many students he deals with regularly. He's teaching those kids and counseling them in the many small and large ways that teachers help guide their students—he's doing it with some nervousness, most likely, but his students probably don't notice it. What does this novice teacher talk about when heading out with friends for an evening? All the usual, no doubt, but it's easy to imagine him talking, too, about the challenges and rewards of teaching—how hard it can be, but how affecting it is to have a third-grader look up at you with real gratitude, or a high schooler (not so much younger than the teacher) learn—incontrovertibly grasp a new truth—before your eyes.

This is a person with prestige in his community of college friends. He is a person who can easily feel good about his choice to be a teacher.

Now, roll forward a year. Our young teacher is getting his sea legs before his own class. He is teaching on his own, with a mentor teacher checking in now and then perhaps, and a little extra support from the principal if the principal has the time and interest. He's solving problems, developing relationships with students, and working through one of the most difficult and rewarding phases in a teacher's life. He's also making an adult salary, though not a particularly large one. He's probably taking courses toward a master's degree in education or related subject in the evenings.

His friends are doing a range of things—taking time off to travel, working in jobs that may be the beginnings of their own careers or may help them learn what they don't want to do for a living, or perhaps they're beginning graduate or professional school. Remember, we're talking about the social circle of the kind of young teacher who should be prized—the talented, ambitious young person. His friends are probably a lot like him—they're people with plenty of options, who are looking for the right paths to exercise their own talents and build meaningful lives. Some are likely to be starting law school or MBA classes; some are taking entry-level business jobs; some are moving back home to their parents to decompress from four years of college, save some money, and consider their choices. Their friend the teacher is probably making as much or more money than most of them. He's probably taking on greater personal challenges in his day-to-day work, and he's working in the public sector, making a difference in the schools that so many commentators spill so much ink over in the newspapers and magazines. He's no underachiever. He looks to the world like a person with a vital and important professional life.

Now look forward another three or four years. Our young teacher's friends are less likely to be business or law students, more likely to be business people and lawyers. Those who took the academic route might well be considering the beginnings of their Ph.D. dissertations. Even those who took the lowest-level business jobs are now likely to be reaching modestly higher rungs on the career ladder. Certainly some of his friends might still be traveling, or still be living at home, working at jobs that aren't panning out and thinking about the right changes to make. But on the whole, our young teacher, who has by now gotten the hang of how to be a classroom educator, and has the skills to walk into class with confidence and break into a lesson without much nervous perspiration, is one of the lower earners among his friends, and probably feels a good deal less like the leader of the pack. "What do you guys do?" someone might ask a table of them at the local pub. "Well, I'm a med student, fourth year." "I'm a lawyer over at Huddle and Pass." "I'm an editor at a national magazine." And our teacher says, "I teach third grade," or "I teach high school biology." No need to feel ashamed, of course. But there's not a lot of prestige for him to grab hold of as he tells his professional story. At the age of twenty-five or so, that may not be a cause for concern.

Roll forward another fifteen years. Our teacher is now forty. His friends are now law partners, business people, doctors, writers, scientists, and professors. Where is he in his career? He could be at the head of a third-grade classroom, teaching the children of some of his first students from student-teacher days. He's probably picked up a doctorate along the way: twenty years of steady night courses have yielded their benefits. And he may well be the happiest of all his friends. In all of their moments of reflection— What kind of contribution am I making? What personal satisfaction am I really getting from my work? What kind of community do I have at work, day to day?—the teacher's answers could be very satisfying. I'm changing lives every day, shaping the minds and souls of my students, he might say. I see the results of my work every day when I look at my students, bump into kids I taught years ago, learn to do my job better every year. And I work in a hive of activity, energized by the youth of the students and the profound purpose of the institutional home we share.

Or maybe he decided to give up teaching. He might have decided at the age of thirty or so that he wanted his children to have the economic advantages he could gain for them through business or law, professions that draw on similar skills and aptitudes. In the business world he could probably triple his salary, though he'd have to trade off the nobility of the educator (and summers off). Or he might have decided that he wanted the greater free-doms of the college professor.

But the most likely ending to this story—not a sad ending by any means—is that we find our teacher in the compromise position of an educational administrator. With his above-average skills and real dedication to the mission of schools, he is now probably a principal, a district-wide curriculum director, or an associate superintendent. What do you do for a living? I'm a lawyer. I'm a VP at Giant Corporation. I'm a high school principal. Or, I'm the head of a school system. That sounds pretty good, and in most cases the money isn't shabby for those jobs.

But what of the classroom teacher? Is there really that much pressure for the most talented teachers to stop teaching, even if they stay in schools? The answer is yes, and I don't think the bigger paychecks for administrators are the main reason. The fact is that the culture of educational administrators is different from the culture of teachers. Walk the floor of the big conferences of principals or superintendents and you find a different feeling from the floor of the larger conferences dedicated to classroom teachers. There's a bit more of an intellectual pitch to the talks and the displays. Certainly there is also more of a managerial pitch too—these are the people who run the practical side of schools and districts. But most striking is the overall feeling that the administrators' conferences are gatherings of people who want to answer larger questions about education—not just how to do it but why, and how educational practice fits in with larger intellectual and policy issues. The classroom teacher looking for the most thoughtful, stimulating professional colleagues will feel the tug of administration for this reason.

The emphasis on credentials in school systems today adds another force to our protagonist's decision to remain in the classroom or to climb the administrative ladder. Teachers are generally awarded higher salaries as they pile up more graduate credits and degrees, and some of the most common degrees for them to earn are degrees in educational administration. The most talented students—those who enjoy learning, who look at graduate courses as a privilege and an opportunity—are the ones who wind up with the credentials to become administrators. And of course the money does exert an influence as well. In many districts, principals earn close to twice what the average teacher earns. Inevitably those who have ability and ambition will think seriously about climbing the ladder to greater money and greater prestige. And that ladder leads right up out of the classroom.

WORK YOU CAN BELIEVE IN

Many of the people I work with at the Great Books Foundation are former K-12 teachers. They are an outstanding bunch—folks who often take a pay cut in order to work with us, who endure the rigors of near-constant travel to bring our message about teaching through discussion and the Socratic method (we call it Shared Inquiry). They lose many of the perks of the teacher's professional schedule (no summers off, no half-days to speak of).

Looking at these people, and at the many more teachers who apply for positions with us, a few characteristics stand out. First, these are not people who are motivated by money. They need enough to get by, certainly, and they deserve professional salaries, but seldom do they base their larger career decisions on compensation. Second, they will work only at what they believe in. This may seem like an obvious trait, but it's rare to see a large group hold this ideal so firmly. I had one key staff member at the foundation insist that she not get paid a bonus tied to our overall success at finding new people to take our training courses and buy our books because, as she said, "It's extremely important for me to know that I'm doing this work as an educator, first and last, and never as a salesman." So she's earning less money in order to preserve her sense of why she does what she does—and this is a single mother of two children.

Perhaps even more important, though, is the tremendous importance the people at our foundation place on whom they work with. They'll take less money; they'll work longer hours; they'll travel beyond most people's endurance. (One colleague showed up at our Chicago office after two days of being trapped in the Baltimore airport because of storms, thrilled to be back but obviously exhausted. "It was just time for me to get back," she said. "Seventeen hours. I rented a car and drove.") But they won't work with colleagues they don't respect. They learn from one another, they help one another think about education and big ideas, and they take tremendous pride in being part of a team of some of the most talented educators in the world. We sometimes joke that some of them would pay us for the privilege of working at the foundation—and we know there's more than a grain of truth to this (more people work as volunteers in our programs around the country than work as paid employees).

The dynamic at work with this group of outstanding educators is the dynamic of self-selection. It's about being part of an elite. It's about a surprising curve that you can show on a graph: when an organization moves from average standards to higher standards, it generally has a harder time finding employees and has to pay them more, because above-average people are a limited commodity. But as an organization's standards go beyond merely above average, as it earns the reputation of being an elite institution where only the most talented people work together, the cost of employment begins to fall. People benefit so much from being part of a known elite, they'll put off the chance to make money in order to get other kinds of compensation—knowledge, pride, and the intangible value of having a notable, elite affiliation.

ANOTHER CASE STUDY

My own personal experience is a case in point, and it is scarcely unique. In the late 1980s and early 1990s I was a full-time graduate student working on a Ph.D. at Columbia University, the father of two daughters, teaching pick-up courses at as many as five different colleges at a time to get by financially. Then I got a big break—the chance to join the faculty at Harvard University with the lowly academic rank of "preceptor." Regardless of the rank, I knew that the affiliation with Harvard would be valuable and would probably lead to better jobs down the road. And of course I'd be inside what many people regard as the finest university in the country.

Three years after I took the job, I left academia to find a way to make more money to support my family. As I built a new professional life, I benefited enormously from having that "Harvard faculty" stamp on my resumé, and from the skills and relationships I developed while at the university. What kind of salary did I earn?

In 1992, my first year at Harvard, I began at a salary of about $26,000—roughly what a token clerk in the New York City subway system made that year, without overtime. I can remember a conversation I had a few years later with a colleague at an Internet company I was working for about my experience teaching at Harvard. The company provided Internet services to schools, and they trotted out my Harvard credential at every public event and sales opportunity I was part of. My colleague had recently been the head of sales for a major computer manufacturer, and he and I once got to talking about salaries. When I told him how much I had made at Harvard, he had a surprising reaction. He didn't believe me. He was genuinely irritated that I wasn't being straight with him. "Really," he said, "what did they pay you?"

He'd probably been making well over $100,000 a year as a sales executive while I was at Harvard, and perhaps several times that. He had imagined, as most people do, that an institution like Harvard would pay its faculty quite well. To a degree, he was right. The full professors on campus did very well, but full professors were and are a small minority of people who teach at Harvard, the mostly older professors who arrive on campus in the middle of astoundingly successful academic careers and are usually quite famous within their special fields. The university employs a teaching corps of young people doing the majority of instruction to undergraduates, and these people earn little money. But they harvest great experience and prestige. I know that in my case, I'd actually have taken even less money. I knew that being at Harvard would be so good for me, that I'd learn so much, that I'd get to see how brilliant colleagues do the same things that I expected to spend my career doing, and that I'd be so proud of the affiliation with that institution that any financial compromise my little family and I could handle would be worthwhile.

Many elite institutions across American public life are driven by the same dynamic. Why else do the most talented lawyers often work for the government at a fraction of what they can earn elsewhere? Why are our universities filled with so many of the best and brightest of our professionals—there to study and teach, making so much less than they could elsewhere? Why else do young doctors (and many not so young) spend years beyond medical school earning small salaries as they train for greater and greater specialization?

And why should our schools not be in the same category? Once we come to believe that they can be, and that we know how to make it so, how can we possibly choose any alternate course? Perhaps out of fairness, one might say. We want our teacher corps to be a humane institution, not to be driven by the competitive fires that ignite even the judicial law clerks and top-drawer graduate students and university lecturers. It's true, we could be fairer to teachers, we could make the profession a little less competitive, a little less demanding. But that's precisely the situation we're in now! And we have discovered that by being fairer to the teachers —particularly to the less talented and less ambitious teachers— we make our students bear the cost, essentially taking from our students to give to our least talented teachers. And of course it's the poor students, whose parents cannot take them out of the schools they are in (because they don't have the money for private schools, or the skills at working the educational bureaucracy for a transfer to a better school) who pay the highest price.

In an era that calls for genuine reform in American education—and our era certainly qualifies—it is high time we begin to change this fact. A tougher apprenticeship period for new teachers is the place to begin. Let us create the expectation that most who begin their careers as teachers won't make the grade, and that those who do will be truly the best and the brightest of every generation, while those who enter the profession and leave in those early years will be proud to say—and will benefit from saying—"I was a teacher."

But even if schools across the nation were to do everything right in their hiring from this day forward, more than three million teachers already in the classroom represent an added challenge. What can we do to support the best among them, to reward them fairly and keep them teaching? What can we do to encourage the weakest among them to step aside and make room for better teachers?

THE COURAGE TO CUT LOOSE THE WORST

After school ended for the year in 2001, Paul Vance, the head of the Washington, D.C., school system, did something shocking. Vance fired 531 teachers—10 percent of the teaching staff in the District of Columbia—with support from Washington's teachers' union. The teachers were dismissed because they failed to meet promises to the school district to provide proof of their qualifications. Some of these teachers had been hired without teaching licenses, and then failed to earn their licenses within the school district's eighteen-month grace period. Others never provided proof of their college degrees. Still others had failed to keep their licenses current through minimal continuing education.

Some of these teachers had come to the D.C. schools through job fairs to fill teaching positions in the toughest schools, schools that most licensed teachers avoid. At the fairs, candidates are given survey sheets to fill out. Went to college? Check the box. Hold a teaching certificate? Check the box. Anxious administrators offered jobs on the spot, credentials to be verified later. Were some of these job candidates faking their resumés? Vance's close review of the D.C. school district's central personnel files made it plain: yes, some were faking. After Vance came into office, blatantly unqualified teachers—and in some cases blatantly fraudulent teachers—were fired. That made news. Far more troubling was the long unreported fact that before this new superintendent took office, so many were allowed to linger within the system for so long.

The single most important step for any school leader to take—getting rid of teachers who do more harm than good to their students—has long been thought impossible. I've heard principals in large urban systems say, sure, they can take a terribly incompetent teacher through the long process of review and appeal, but the investment of time in that process isn't wise. The average principal today stays in his or her job for only four years. Many are aware of that ticking clock as they go about trying to make their schools better, and they choose to push poor teachers off to the side rather than invest the great amount of time they think will be necessary to get rid of these teachers. Better, many think, to focus on new programs, new strategies, or new facilities that may lift all boats, even those of the poor kids stuck with the rotten teachers.

In the long run this might make sense. At the level of averages and aggregates, there is an appealing logic here. But students live their lives in the short run. They are merely life-size, distinct indi-viduals, not averages or aggregates. Of the nation's more than 3 million teachers, if only 1 of 20 does a particularly poor job, but stays in place, it means that some 150,000 bad teachers are filling the days of 3 million students. That is the measure of the harm done by thinking in averages and aggregates.

Assume that every school is home to at least a few outstand-ing teachers—an assumption I've seen borne out in uncounted schools across the country, urban, rural, and suburban; rich, poor, and in between. How do these professionals react to their weakest colleagues? How are they affected by colleagues who say things to students like this: "While you do these worksheets, I'm going to make $50,000 a year sitting next to the window and reading my newspaper"; "If you can't shape up please leave school now"; and the cutting self-criticism I have heard from too many teachers, "I don't care"? Teachers who speak this way to their students tend to cluster in the worst-off schools, schools with the poorest students and the weakest administrators, though one or two can be found in even the very best public schools. They are a part of the American educational landscape, and their very presence lowers the sights of principals who seek positive change.

The magic of Washington, D.C., Superintendent Vance's act— the aspect of this story that may lead superintendents throughout the country to wonder whether perhaps they too can finally act against the most harmful of their teaching staff—is that he went ahead and did it. The laws and regulations restricting a school system's ability to cut loose teachers who obviously fail at their jobs are onerous but, as Vance's move reminds us, not impossible. The fact that the Washington teachers' union has not opposed the firings in principle (though the union is challenging a small number of individual cases) is remarkable, and may suggest more union support for similar housecleaning in other districts.

The *Washington Post* reported that Barbara Bullock, president of the Washington teachers' union, "said that dismissing the teachers was management's right. She said some teachers may have extenuating circumstances but that others do not have legitimate excuses. 'When you came into the system, you knew you had your requirements to make,' Bullock said. 'It's just like lawyers and doctors—you have a bar to pass. We expect to have qualified teachers in the classroom.'" Bullock seems to understand that the best teachers are too often driven out by the worst. She and other union leaders are beginning to act on that knowledge. In addition to seeking higher salaries and better contracts for their members, they are more and more willing to allow school leaders to free good teachers from their most embarrassing colleagues.

HOW MUCH MEDIOCRITY?

But what of the middle ground, the teachers who are not excellent but not screamingly awful? They don't commit crimes. Their teaching licenses are in order. But if your child were a student in one of their classes, you'd have the feeling of opportunities to learn being missed every day. In most schools, everyone knows who these weaker teachers are. A Seattle parent whose child had just such a teacher described for the *Seattle Times* how her daughter, who "used to love school and wanted to be a teacher," reacted. She "cries on Mondays now," the mother reported, "complains of stomachaches and says she wants to be home-schooled. The principal's assured me I'll get the good teacher next year, but what do I do, write off this year?" In uncounted thousands of schools, students and parents are given exactly that advice. Make the best of it. Do what you can. Be patient. Wait until next year.

This patience works to the advantage of school systems: they get to wait out weak teachers and avoid the burdensome work of forcing poor teachers to improve or leave. Of course, most school districts spend a great deal of money on teacher professional development, and they do make great efforts to help teachers teach better. But at the end of the day, varying degrees of failure at that task are the norm. "What you end up with," admits Paul Houston, executive director of the American Association of School Administrators, "is a certain amount of mediocrity being permitted." And without a doubt a certain amount of mediocrity will *always* be permitted. But how much?

To force out mediocrity, we must do three things. First, we must insist on recruiting only the very best applicants for teaching positions. Second, we must create a probationary period during which the best new recruits earn their place in the teaching profession; recruits cannot expect to remain just by avoiding striking incompetence. And third, we must concentrate professional development dollars and hours on a small number of goals rather than offering generic "continuing professional education credits" for any and all seminars, trips, or classes that in-service teachers may take. Each of these three steps is a great challenge. Hiring only the best applicants is perhaps the most straight-forward of the three. Raising the bar for probationary periods for new teachers is tougher. Changing in-service professional development may be the most difficult of all.

According to the U.S. Department of Education, nationally only about 2 percent of new teachers are not hired in permanent positions when their initial probation ends. But the city of Toledo, Ohio, is a pioneer in a taking a tougher and smarter view of new-teacher probation. Through a new program there, veteran teachers get to know new recruits and play an important role in approving most of them for long-term positions and in screening out the weakest among them. About 10 percent of new teachers in Toledo don't make it past probation, a big step in the right direction. But what about the teachers who are better than the worst, but not as good as they should be? (Imagine the recruiting poster: New Quality Standards for Our Schoolchildren! From this day forward, only the top 90 percent of new teachers will make the grade!) The courage that our schools still lack, even in Toledo, is the courage to say that we want only the best new teachers to make a long-term career in the classroom.

Today most school districts spend between $1,000 and $2,000 per teacher per year on professional development, including paid speakers who work with teachers on the no-school-days and half-days that parents often scratch their heads about ("Another half-day? Why on earth?"). But a great deal of this professional development is scattershot. Frequently it is provided by staff of textbook publishers, who may not be able to resist the temptation to skew training toward the publisher's goals. They help teachers develop strategies for using the books they have sold to schools—a good thing to do, but these teacher-trainers often measure their success by how many new books a school buys after the training, rather than teachers' and students' performance.

Aside from the textbook people, professional development is often delivered by consultants who get paid by the day. They often develop one-shot training routines that they perform for teachers, and they have great incentive to deliver more or less the same presentation to widely different groups of teachers. Most school districts also have their own full-time professional development staff, which allows for sustained attention to district training goals, an expensive but vital commitment.

The central problem of professional development, no matter who provides it, is focus. Most districts devote between twenty and forty hours per teacher each year on professional development, but the U.S. Department of Education reports that 85 percent of teachers receive fewer than eight hours per year of professional development in a specific area. So a math teacher in a district that supports forty professional development hours a year is likely to spend fewer than eight of those hours learning about teaching math better. The rest of those hours will be scattered among other subjects, ranging from test-taking tips for students to the most efficient ways to fill out report cards.

Even full-time professional development staff are often hampered in their work by demands from the top for short-term outcomes. Rising student test scores are the coin of the realm in teacher professional development, and it takes unusual fortitude for a principal to resist putting pressure on teachers to focus on short-run results. Far better, of course, would be to measure the change in *teachers*, in their ability to communicate honestly, to experiment beneficially, and to connect with students as individuals. "The hardest part of working with teachers over time," says one principal in Chicago, "is having faith in the long term. My best teachers today, they got that good because of things that happened years ago. Can I put my time and budget into laying the foundation for these new young teachers the same way? Can I say, Let's not think about the scores this year, let's just do what's right to shape these educators for the long haul? Man, oh, man, I'm trying. But if my kids' scores don't go up *this* year, I'll be looking for a new job myself."

5

Why Lasting Change
Always Comes from the
Bottom Up and the
Inside Out

School superintendents have difficult jobs. In addition to attending to the inner workings of their school districts, they
need to report to various officials and political leaders, and to the
general public. Typically they don't last long in their jobs. According to the Council of Great City Schools, superintendents in larger
American cities stay in their jobs fewer than three years on average. Teachers, on the other hand, tend to stay in their jobs for
many years once they have made it through their initial probationary periods. More than 65 percent of teachers in the United
States have been on the job longer than ten years; about 30 per-

cent for more than twenty years. The difference in stability is pretty much constant as you move up the ladder in school. On average, teachers stay in their jobs longer than principals do; principals stay longer than mid-level administrators; and mid-level administrators stay longer than superintendents.

On the surface, then, better to invest resources in making change at the classroom level than to bet on top-down change, because at the classroom level teachers are likely to stay in schools longer than the administrators who populate the upper ranks of school systems. Teachers who stick around can keep change going; top-down change is often crippled by advocates for particular reform strategies who duck out just as programs begin to gain traction. But there's more to the rapid turnover of high-level administrators than meets the eye. Not only does that turnover frustrate top-down change; the turnover is itself the result of a number of underlying forces that often short-circuit large-scale, system-level change.

DISTANCE

One of these forces is distance, both real and figurative. In most school districts, school buildings are home to students, teachers, and the support and administrative staff who work there. Somewhere else in a town a building called something like "the central office" houses the senior administrators, who work within a very different culture than school-based staff. The central office usually feels like a place run by grown-ups. Less formal than a law office, it nevertheless manages to fill its halls with a sense of seriousness. Schools, of course, are dominated by the throngs of children who come and go all day, vastly outnumbering the grown-ups. In the typical school building there is no place, not even the principal's inner office, that the physical presence of students—their voices, the very vibrations of their feet in the halls—does not reach. As a dramatic consequence, everything that happens in a school building, every policy, every program, every plan, is shaped to at least some degree by that pervasive presence of actual students. Administrative office buildings are profoundly different. Often quiet, they feel like the bureaucratic retreats they are.

Schools are hectic, stressful places. Adults who work there, whether or not they get along with one another, generally feel a sense of common purpose, even common sacrifice, because of that stress and intensity. Other adults who happen to stop by— including central office staff and outside consultants—generally stand out. Similarly, change that begins in the school is local, familiar, even partisan to the cause of that particular building. Change that begins in the central office feels distant.

The *New York Times* describes that city's central office headquarters this way:

> The 14-floor stone and masonry building at 110 Livingston Street was built in 1925 by McKim, Mead and White, the architectural firm that also built the old Pennsylvania Station. It originally housed the Benevolent and Protective Order of Elks, and was not taken over by the Board of Education until 1939. Since then, it has become one of the few buildings, like 1600 Pennsylvania Avenue, 1 Police Plaza, and 10 Downing Street, that is immediately identifiable to New Yorkers by its address alone. Since the New York City fiscal crisis of the

mid-70's, the building has grown increasingly dilapidated, along with the schools it serves, and it has turned into a monument to almost every allegation of failure that has been heaped upon the larger public school system.

In that building toil hundreds of administrators set to the task of planning reforms for New York City's one thousand schools. How could their work possibly avoid the taint of a building that has become a monument to failure? How could their work possibly resist the culture and climate of the central office building? How could it speak the language of the classroom when it transpires in a building absent of students, absent of working teachers, but filled with hundreds upon hundreds of planners, coordinators, supervisors, and clerks?

In the small town of Marblehead, Massachusetts, the school system's headquarters occupies a converted home hidden on a large lot behind an acre of dense trees. Local children say it's a haunted house. It seems distant to the students, far away and scary, because students never go there. It's an outpost, literally hidden away from the town's children, families, and schools. Can reform initiatives coming from this building avoid seeming to be the issue of spirits haunting the old home?

In Gig Harbor, Washington, as in many towns, the school headquarters occupies a converted school that became available as the town's school-age population dwindled in the 1970s. It's a place so obviously meant for children that the lack of young people within its walls is vivid. Small architectural details—room in the hallways for lockers, bathrooms built for children—leave the visitor expecting to hear a bell ring and the hallways fill with students. But that never happens; the children are missing.

These three buildings, different from one another, have in common the fact of estrangement from the ordinary life of schools, and in that they are typical of the places where large-scale school reform is managed. They are literally distant from classrooms, and with that physical distance come other kinds of distance that cripple the prospects of reform. Administrators are generally years removed from daily classroom work, and their standards of success are dramatically different from most teachers'. Victory for many administrators takes the form of annual test scores, enrollment data, and graduation percentages while teachers generally measure success in terms of a good day, a student lit up with knowledge, or a comment from a student that sends the message, *Yes, I understand, I'm learning*. Reform that works over time works at this level, the level of one class, one student, one moment at a time. The more removed they are from these small facts, the less likely that reform efforts will succeed.

SPEED

Another of the underlying forces that frustrates top-down change is speed, or, to be more precise, lack of speed. Teachers work hard every day to respond to the captive energies of rooms filled with students: the pace in a classroom is naturally fast. A new idea can be brought to a class instantly; new experiments in how to present class material often erupt in "real time." With a couple of days' planning, hours of new, carefully thought-out material can make their way into class. But administrators, by definition, don't spend their days responding to the rapid-fire intelligence of children. Instead, most of them work in offices. They typically talk to people on the phone more often than face-to-face, and they need time to build support for new ideas—the support of superiors, peers, and subordinates. The effective administrator deploys craftiness, knowledge of the system, favors due, and alliances cultivated over time to make change happen. And that all takes time.

"Here's what happens when I get a good idea, something like a small little thing that teachers could do in their classes that would make things better for the kids," says a superintendent in a suburban district in the Midwest. "First, I talk to my deputy about it. If it seems like a really great idea and she's behind it, then I talk to two principals I trust, and if they're behind it, then I talk to some parents who I think have some discretion and will tell me whether they think it's a rotten idea before they start forming a committee to oppose it before it even exists. So, this process has taken a couple of months already.

"Next, I sit down and write a two-page summary of how this new idea could work just at a very high level, and then I pass that to my deputy who fills in the details of how it would work for elementary versus high school, special education, Title I, bilingual education, and all the rest. Then it goes to the attorney who vets it for federal and state policy violations. If it's still alive at that point—and this is what, six months later?—then I try to find a champion. In almost all cases, I never want to present an idea to our school board as my idea, because part of my job is to be the bad guy on some issues, like the need to spend money on things, and so my standing with the board will complicate any good idea if I'm the one who says it's my idea. The best champion, of course, is a board member, so I try to find someone who will fall in love with this idea to take it up and do a little presentation to the board.

"If the board loves it, maybe they'll warm up to having a line item to fund it in the following year's budget. If they like it but don't love it, then I have to go find someone else to pay for it in the community. If they're lukewarm or worse, it's dead. But let's say it's alive, for the sake of argument. Now I have to tell all my principals and teachers about this idea, I have to hold their hands in how to implement it, and then I have to watch them do it to make sure it's done right. So we're at least two years down the road now from my great new idea, and we're just getting started. This is the reason why I try hard not to have too many good ideas."

Time, of course, is not necessarily a bad thing in the making of change, but the history of school reform suggests that bad ideas surface just as regularly as good ones. Time conspires to keep the bad ones afloat longer in the world of the school system administrators than is possible in the classroom. The teacher trying out a new idea gets immediate feedback. The new idea worked, didn't work, or came out somewhere in the middle. A good teacher absorbs the lesson, recalibrates his or her approach, and refines the idea at hand. Administrators generally don't have the luxury of that kind of constant feedback. So much more time goes into building support for the very first attempts at deploying change of any scale throughout a system that by the time initial results filter back in, a great deal of time (and, likely, patience) has been spent. Bottom-up brings with it the virtue of a fast cycle of experiment;

top-down is always slower, more or less in proportion to how high toward the top the change begins.

Bottom-up change works because *change happens first*. Change must then fight its way upstream to become official, and the full range of complications ensues. But even if bottom-up change dies as it moves upward, the fact that the whole process has begun with something good happening—actually *happening* in a real classroom with real students—is profound. Beyond the virtues of the specific bit of change at hand, teachers and students become used to the notion that things can be made better, that individuals and their small dreams matter a great deal, and that the system does not take precedence over the classroom.

More than one grand political theory, from more than one end of the political spectrum, has been built on this simple notion of the virtue of bottom-up change. Friedrich Hayek, the economist, countered John Maynard Keynes's arguments for active government intervention in economic markets with his own theory that placed the greatest virtue in the actions of as large a number as possible of individuals striking out independently to create economic gain. The government economists trusted under Keynes's model to shape economic order would generally come up with a relatively narrow range of ideas. Hayek's model of change proposed instead that the competition of ideas from the masses of ordinary people, some trained but many not, would result in the long run in better ideas, because of a richer set of ideas input at the beginning of the process.

Essentially Hayek was saying that those who were *chosen* for power could never govern as well as the very best from among the ordinary masses—who were best because in the tumultuous competition of ideas, theirs had *proven* best. Hayek was thinking specifically of government economists selected for their posts because of their education and political alliances; in the case of centralized school reform, designated school administrators and other official reformers play a similar role. Ideas that triumph in a contest open to a large and unfiltered body of people will always trump those that emerge from a narrow, preselected group. Although Hayek was celebrated as a hero of the political right, a very similar idea was summed up in the slogan that Chairman Mao offered to critics during a period of liberalization in China: "Let a thousand schools of thought contend; let a thousand flowers bloom."

Hayek and Mao—an odd couple if ever there was one—jointly point to a wise path for school reform: rather than placing big bets on a few ideas that emerge from experts and school district leaders, allow reform to bubble up from thousands of small innovations. Let them vie with one another for the privilege of moving upstream, from bottom to top.

Apply these ideas to schools and you wind up with a clear mandate to cultivate new ideas at the classroom level and to create pathways for those ideas to percolate up, competing with other new ideas for better education. Let the most effective ideas carry the day. Rexford G. Brown sums up the argument for bottom-up reform in his book *Schools of Thought*:

> There are no secrets here. If you want young people to think, you ask them hard questions and let them wrestle with the answers. If you want them to analyze something or interpret it or evaluate it, you ask them to do so and show them how

to do it with increasing skill. If you want them to approach interesting or difficult problems, you give them interesting or difficult problems and help them develop a conscious repertoire of problem-solving strategies. If you want them to think the way scientists or historians or mathematicians do, you show them how scientists and historians and mathematicians think, and you provide opportunities for them to practice and compare those ways of thinking.

In every school we visited, someone knew what to do and practiced it to some degree. Great teachers have always known how to make students think about and apply their knowledge. But seldom did we see the *majority* of teachers in a school practicing or stimulating a literacy of thoughtfulness.

There are no secrets, Brown says, but somehow the good things going on in some classrooms are not making their way to the rest of the representative schools that Brown and his colleagues studied. His phrase "someone knew what to do" rings out. It is true everywhere. There is always an island of ability of thoughtfulness, of excellence. The challenge for people who want to help schools improve is not so much to bring new seeds to fallow fields, or, like missionaries, to bring a new gospel to people living without hope for Heaven. Instead it is to help the best that is already happening in every school spread up and down every hallway, and to keep that process of improvement continuing forever.

One middle school in Washington State that I've visited ran a school improvement program built directly on these principles. The school sits on the edge of the town center in a small city; an old factory, producing nothing today and largely abandoned, sits partway up a hill visible throughout the town, though upscale shops catering to weekend travelers from Seattle and beyond suggest a postindustrial future that may be brighter than the recent past. The student body is diverse, including American Indian students from a nearby reservation, Latino students whose parents work in the hotels and restaurants on the Pacific shore, and the sons and daughters of area professionals who live in large hilltop Victorian homes. Each grade has three classes, and each teacher is asked to fill out a brief form every Friday afternoon listing new good ideas that surfaced in the classroom that week. Every month the teachers take two hours to sit together and review their reports.

The principal, a youthful woman new to the area when she took the job three years ago, does not expect this simple program to work miracles, but she has seen strong and steady results from it. "Two good things are happening here because of the weekly sheets," she says. "First, the teachers pay more attention to each other, and think more like a team. This is a simple tool, kind of artificial even, but there are a lot of teachers who don't have the time or energy to talk much with their colleagues, and this makes that happen on a regular basis. The second good thing is that they pay more attention to what they do. If you ask them to write down their good ideas, they really do wind up having more good ideas. And the ideas *are* good ones—that's the official goal of this thing, and it's very important. I've had teachers write out new ways of teaching math to advanced students—stuff that could be published in teaching journals, it's so good and innovative—and teachers coming up with better ways to reward and discourage behavior, and lots and lots of practical time-management advice. There's more here, in this process, than in any program I've seen in ten years of running schools that came from any central office."

A recently retired superintendent goes even further as he makes the case for bottom-up change. "Picture yourself as a new superintendent. You come in and you have maybe a thousand teachers in your district. You've got about two hundred real stars—man, these people can teach. You give them a class, and they're doing the research, buying the books, going to conferences, and then you stand them up in front of the kids and they lock in. It's the Vulcan mind meld. They're just great at what they do. Then you have the two hundred at the bottom. They stink. They're not trying, and even if they did try, they're not really that good anyway.

"In the middle you've got your six hundred average Joes. If you gave them extra years toward their retirement, they'd be gone tomorrow. They're not driven by passion for their work as teachers, though many of them once were. They give you a good day's work for a day's pay. They do what you require of them, not much more, not much less. You have an even chance with them to put great materials in their hands, plug them into district programs that structure what they do, monitor how they do it, and the kids they teach will do okay. In my life as a superintendent, there's no question that the most good I've done for students was to get that middle group working a little bit better than they otherwise would. The only reason you need these district programs is to move teachers from the middle of the pile up toward the top. And that's some trick—it's mighty hard to do. I've done it a few times, but not consistently.

"The path that works is to find ways to segment the teachers in each building so that the best in the building get the levers of control to work with the others, to get them in gear to the extent they can, and to reach around them to the kids. This is kind of exciting—you see a program get that spark that's going to make it work when you see two or three of the really bright teachers in a building get behind it and start talking to the others. You can't really force it; you have to let it build with its own logic in every building, because it's really a social logic. The teachers who become champions in any new program are the ones who use their relationships with the average-Joe teachers to put a little pressure on them to care a little more about this, and to put the effort in to make it work. Then, if you can get a couple of strong parents into the mix, you know you've got a winner. The teachers who resist a good new program, who resist doing the better jobs they could be doing, will really be like a stone wall with their kids, and they might not be much better with their colleagues, but it's so hard to keep that front up with a couple of parents who they know are there as volunteers, there to look out for their kids' interests.

"And they know the other secret about parents in a school. If you can get a couple of parents who care about something in the school to start coming regularly to the building, they don't stop till their kids graduate. The parents that can make that commitment to start coming, they're just so hard to fight that a teacher who's looking for the path of least resistance will stop fighting them, and just get with the program now and then. I've seen it happen—not often, but I've seen it. You get those two or three teachers who really spark, and you get two or three parents working with them, and that becomes the engine in a school that a principal can use to get a hell of a lot done. Good things will come from that.

"So you can invent or buy district-level programs, and sometimes they're great. But if you can fix the way teachers and parents work in their schools, you'll get better results. Get any random group of people together and you'll see, obviously, that some are leaders. Let them lead, help them lead, and the group works better. The same dynamic is true among teachers. If the district takes away the chance for the natural leaders among teachers to lead, if it gives all the teachers instructions and says 'Do this,' that's just a massive missed opportunity. Far better to go to the best teachers and ask questions. So it's not, Do This, but, What are *you* doing that's exciting? That's a magic question. Get the parents into the equation too, show them that the best teachers are on to some strong ideas and need their help to make them real, and you've got a winning model. You've got the possibility of real change. You've got some hope."

That hope is a democratic kind of hope. It lives in rich schools and poor schools, among students born in the United States and those from other nations, and it certainly lives equally among black students, white students, and students of every shade and background. It lives in the suburbs, the small towns, and the inner cities.

This last point comes as a surprise to many. "But what about the poor schools?" I'm often asked when I talk about supporting teachers and ending the waste of billions of dollars on large-scale, top-down reform. "What about the inner-city schools? The ghetto schools? The deprived students? What about the underprivileged?" There are a hundred ways to phrase this question, but the assumption underlying it is always the same: better teachers will make a big difference for middle-class kids, for white kids, for kids who work hard and perform—that is, better teachers will make a big difference for *us*, but what about *them*? The answer to this very complicated question is quite simple: what is best for *us* is best for *them* too.

Schools, alas, are limited. We cannot make poor students rich. We cannot make dangerous streets safe. We cannot turn the sons and daughters of laborers into the sons and daughters of doctors and lawyers. But schools are also hugely powerful. Our job is not to make the poor rich and the dangerous safe, or to turn the children of the masses into the children of the elites. Our job is to teach, and to teach well. That we can do, which in itself can seem more of a miracle than all of the false and foolish aspirations some would foist upon schools.

"THE KIDS ARE GREAT"

Many teachers do not wish to teach in the toughest inner-city schools, but the same dynamics that turn off teachers in the suburbs are most to blame in the inner cities as well. "It's not the kids. The kids are great," says one veteran Los Angeles teacher. "Sometimes they're scary, sometimes they're heartbreaking, but they're always worth coming back to. It's the conditions that bring you down. It's the toilets that don't work. The clocks in the hallway that stopped ten years ago. And it's being at the bottom of the barrel. The teachers at my school are mostly ones who don't have a choice in transferring out. They've made enemies in the system, or they screwed up somewhere and the other principals know it, or they just don't care, they want to hide till they hit their pension. They're worse than the toilets."

A Boston teacher has his own take on teaching in the inner city. "There are a lot of great teachers here, but a lot of clock punchers too," he says. "You get the feeling sometimes that this school is the place bad teachers come to die. But some of us see it differently. This is where we want to be. You know, my daughter transferred over into my school from her high school in the suburbs. Even after all the stories she heard me tell—or maybe it was more because of those stories. She wanted to be in the real world, to be with the kids whose lives weren't as easy as the kids in that school she was at before, kids who have that crazy spark from making it in a tough place. She likes that. I like that too. So I keep coming back. That's the secret, you know, to making it in these schools. You have to keep coming back. We get these young people from the Peace Corps, from Teach for America, from the mayor's office, from other programs. They come in for a couple of months and quit. They come sometimes for a few weeks for some special thing they're doing, then they leave. The kids can smell that. They see who's going to stay, who has the commitment. That's when they can start learning. So my advice to these young people who start teaching here and don't win the war in the first afternoon, or the first month, or even the first year, I just tell them to keep coming back. That's how you win."

Rich Geib taught at Berendo Middle School in Los Angeles in the early 1990s. "I was hired initially to take the place of a veteran teacher," he writes in a powerful tale on his web page of his brief tenure at the often violent middle school. "The class had suffered through a series of ineffectual substitute teachers by the time I finally arrived. When I told them I was their new permanent teacher, they answered, '*Yeah! Sure! You're just another sub!*'" They were sure Geib would not stay, but he did, at least for a few years. That skepticism—enough to lead many teachers to ask whether they are poor substitutes for something better, no matter their "permanent" teaching assignments—is almost universal in the toughest schools. The students expect little commitment from teachers.

What does it take to turn around a falling inner-city school? The same rare qualities that rural and suburban schools need to change—respect and support for teachers, a willingness to experiment, and administrative leadership ready to be advocates for students and teachers. Inner-city teachers who approach their teaching as a series of endless experiments do better than teachers who try to perform old teaching scripts. Inner-city teachers who treat their students as individuals do better than those who relate to their classes as undifferentiated masses of students. Inner-city teachers who listen carefully to what their students say and care about what their students think do better than teachers who can't or won't take their students' ideas seriously.

WHAT TEACHERS DO AND SAY

Do poor inner-city students perform better with no-frills curricula? Some educators think so, but there are as many success stories in the inner cities built around rich learning strategies and demands for high-level critical thinking as there are "back to basics" models for tough city schools. Some years, in some districts, back-to-basics is all the rage. Other years, critical thinking comes back into vogue. What matters most is what teachers do and say with their students, not the high-level models that schools choose. Two outstanding inner-city education programs make this clear.

Fresno County, California, lies between Los Angeles and San Francisco, and even when those cities boom, Fresno tends to struggle. Youa Her, a seventeen-year-old high school junior, is a typical student in Fresno. A recent immigrant living in a family of eleven, Youa left Vietnam when she was four and found her way to California a few years later. After having trouble in a more traditional high school in Fresno, Youa found herself enrolled in the Center for Advanced Research and Technology, a vocational school for high school juniors and seniors. CART, as the school is known, was launched with the financial support of local businesses and is big news in the Clovis Unified School District. Courses are nontraditional—they concentrate on technical subjects, and many involve internships in local technology-based businesses. Youa attends CART with the children of Mexican migrants, recent gang members, and students from some of the poorest areas in the state. But her school is safe, and the feeling of community there is strong.

"Coming to America was a big change for me," she told *Teacher Magazine* for a story about the school. "When I started school the only three [phrases] I knew in English were 'yes,' 'no,' and 'Please can I go to the bathroom?' I used to cry all the time doing my homework because no one was there to help me. Now, I'm better with my learning skills and everything; my grades are up big time. I appreciate this place so much."

What has CART done to help students like Youa Her succeed?

Their curriculum may be part of the story, but more important than the specifics of the curriculum is the fact that it is innovative. All the students at CART know that they're living inside an experiment, and that the world is watching them. That feeling of importance works wonders among the poverty of Fresno just as it does among the suburbs of San Francisco. The technological hardware is wonderful to have, but the magic at CART comes from the teachers and the students, not from the machines. Before CART opened for its first class of students, "the job of designing the courses was left to CART's first crop of teachers," *Teacher Magazine* reported. The teachers have chosen a flexible track for their courses. After September 11, 2001, technology-design teachers gave their students an unexpected, real-life challenge: design and install a new video security system for the school. It was not an exercise; what the students produced in their class would have a direct impact on all their lives.

So, is the secret of CART's success to be found in the pervasive presence of technology? Hardly. CART's success is more a matter of the enthusiasm of the teachers, their willingness to experiment in the larger project of CART and within their own classes, and the feeling up and down the hallways that the students are being asked real questions (questions like, How do we design a security system? What do we mean by security? What limits do we want to impose on the privacy of citizens of our school?), and that their answers will have a real impact on their lives and the lives of others.

Rich Geib tells the story of what happens when technological hardware is left to carry the load of school improvement without support for, and from, outstanding teachers. At Berendo Middle

School, "we teachers were herded into the school auditorium and told by the administration that this dynamic new computer technology would enable these underachieving young people to achieve, where every previous innovation had failed. But after an expensive computer lab was installed on campus, the predictable result was atrocious writing printed out cleanly on laser printers decorated with clever background digital imagery." When technology enters schools as part of a top-down improvement strategy, much less is possible than when teachers are the leading force, advocating, planning, and delivering new technology programs like the programs that CART has put at the heart of a remarkable school.

Another remarkable program for the toughest inner-city students takes a radically different approach to reaching troubled young (and old) people. The Clemente Humanities Course was developed by the writer Earl Shorris to bring the kinds of traditional humanities study usually found in college classics departments to inner-city students, many of them former convicts and some still in jail, hoping to complete their high school equivalency degrees and perhaps go on to college. Shorris has no interest in the kind of preprofessional learning that seems to make CART such a success. For him, the humanities—literature and art about the nature of men and women—are the root of power for the poor.

Shorris is a contradiction: a conservative radical. He believes in hard-study, old-style culture and disciplined thinking precisely because they make the poor more powerful. The rich remain rich, he says, because they understand the stories, histories, and habits of men and women through the ages. "Where freedom found its first clear expression, in ancient Athens," he writes in his book about the Clemente Course, *Riches for the Poor*, "the separation of the humanities from the public world was not possible; the humanities and the polis needed each other for their very existence."

A university-educated white man of great learning, Shorris approaches his students, all poor, with enormous respect: "If they were not understood as cases to be managed, if one could sit at the feet of the poor, and listen; if one could be a student at the school of their lives, of what had befallen them, was there not something more to be learned?" With respect like this for students in the worst schools, any teacher can find at least some success. Like the staff at CART, Shorris believes that the root of his success lies in his program's curriculum. Perhaps. But a far more likely source of success is the combination of high standards, personal respect, and emphasis on teaching through Socratic dialogue that is at the heart of the Clement Course.

Shorris describes what he's up to in the Clemente Course this way: "The case for the humanities as a radical antidote to long-term poverty rests finally on the question of who is born human and to what extent a person is capable of enjoying his or her humanity. Pericles faced the question as it applied to the citizens of Athens, and he responded that all citizens were capable of noble deeds, 'nor does poverty bar the way; if a man is able to serve the state, he is not hindered by the obscurity of his condition.'" We might choose to modernize Pericles' language and talk more about serving the public good, but clearly the faith that both Shorris and Pericles have in abundance is the very faith that teachers of the poor need—the faith that every student can make a contribution to our society. That is the great motive to learn—not merely to benefit personally but to serve the broader community. Teachers who look to their students in inner-city schools and see only wards of the state, burdens, and criminals are blind to the dignity that Pericles saw in the wretchedly poor of Athens, and which all good teachers see in their students.

That vision, the unique view of the individual teacher, can help reshape American education far more profoundly than any school reform program. Students always test their teachers, and teachers too seldom pass those tests. What they are looking for in their teachers are a few basic qualities—honesty, integrity, concern. They generally dislike teachers who merely parrot what their own superiors, or their own lesson plans, tell them to say. They respond to the local, not to the imperial. They respond to the individual, not to the institution. They respond to the act of one man or woman stepping away from the protection of the school system and the textbook, from the collusion of adults and authorities, and taking risks based on faith in individual students. That act of faith, the faith of one teacher in one student, is the center of it all.

6

How to Make Change—
Some Do's and Don'ts for
Teachers, Administrators,
and Parents

This book began with an argument against the conventional thrust of school reform—fix the system, change the standards, impose new structures. I have argued instead for a bottom-up approach to education, insisting that the best way to fix the whole is to fix the smallest pieces that make up the whole. Put more simply, start with the classroom and the teacher, and when we've made each one as good as it can be, the whole system will be vastly improved and that improvement will endure. It is only fair to ask the obvious question: how, specifically, do we do this? The answers to this question—and there is not one answer, there are many—are different for teachers, school administrators, parents, and citizens.

TEACHERS AT THE ROOT

The "three do's and one don't" I've outlined earlier are at the heart of what teachers can best contribute to improving their classrooms. If they focus on individuals, emphasize honest communication and dialogue with their students ("keeping it real"), and always find ways to experiment with and in their classes ("making it new"), their classes will have a vitality and freshness that too few have today. As for the big "don't," most teachers understand that their classrooms are better served by attending to the concrete wonders that their students bring to school every day—the questions, the ideas, the challenges; the anger, the hopes, the horrors—than by trying to win the large philosophical and bureaucratic battles of school reform. The small facts of the classroom are far more important than the large abstractions of the education business that teachers are too often asked to drape around their day-to-day plans and activities. Avoid the fads of educationalists and professional reformers; make the classroom a stage for the wonder of ordinary human curiosity and social life, and much good will be done.

Three teachers I've been lucky enough to know stand out as remarkably good examples of teachers who are doing their all to make their classrooms better than most. Michael Wagner has taught junior high school social studies for almost thirty years in Brooklyn, New York. Wagner generally wears the look of a man with a joke in mind, but his expression reveals more wonder than humor. He sees unexpected things all around him. He works hard to keep his eyes and ears from falling into the habits that block out most of what we see and hear. Wagner never seems to seek to confirm the expected; instead he works hard at noticing what most people fail to notice. He never seems to dismiss anything as extraneous.

In his eighth-grade American history test, Wagner includes questions about student-produced work that he teaches as core texts in his classroom. Students profile historical figures, plan new cities, and try to solve social problems with public policies. The work they produce often lands in the hands of their classmates, alongside the work of Thomas Jefferson and Thomas Paine. Wagner's point is not to say that the student work is as good or as important as the writing of our nation's founders. Rather, he pays attention to his students' work out of ordinary respect. "Look at what these kids are doing," he says. "It's just remarkable. It deserves attention." Wagner has managed to overcome one of the greatest challenges that confronts every teacher: he sees his students as individuals and respects them just as much as he would if he were not their teacher. He sees their work as more than a response to his assignments; he sees it as the labor of actual individuals. He sees it as you or I might see the work of someone we've never met who hands us an essay and says, Please tell me what you think of this.

Another teacher worth emulating taught high school English classes in a number of small New England towns beginning in the 1980s. She enjoys describing some of the writing exercises she cooked up for her students. She'd bring in cows' brains from the butcher, lay them on a classroom table, and have the students write about what they saw and why it mattered. She would begin a class by throwing a chair across the room, and then have the students describe what she had done and speculate about why. She found hundreds of ways to engage her students' minds and feelings, and get them writing. Over time, though, her philosophy as a teacher changed, and she began to feel that she was doing too much for her students, offering them more entertainment than practical help in tackling their own intellectual challenges. She decided they would learn more important lessons about writing if they wrote about the things they cared about most. So her methods changed, and her classrooms became less dramatic. They began to resemble writing workshops. Students would come to class to work on long-term writing projects about their own deepest interests, some academic, some personal.

Her new approach was distinctly different from her old one, and the kind and quality of her students' work changed. Still, I suspect that she overestimates the importance of her specific teaching approach for the long run. Regardless of whether her students are writing about the crazy teacher throwing a chair or their own personal fascination with fast cars, they are lucky enough to have a teacher who thinks deeply about how she teaches, cares about making a difference in her students' intellectual lives, and is always experimenting with new methods of teaching. Those are the qualities that matter most. Teaching with method A instead of method B makes much less of a difference than having a teacher who cares about and questions all her teaching methods, who teaches thoughtfully and constantly tries to make her classroom practices better.

Michael Haradon, a teacher in a Phoenix high school, is another teacher worth emulating. He does not throw chairs, and he does not, as a rule, assign students to study one another's work. In fact, his school's curriculum is built around one-on-one instruction. Haradon's particular genius is his ability to listen to students. When he sits with students—and with adults—he always asks them a lot of questions and listens to their replies with obvious curiosity and respect. He does not listen for correct answers. He does not work from the beginning of a lesson plan to the end. Instead he listens to his students' ideas, as he would with a friend or a colleague, and responds to what they say in a manner that generally surprises new students. Immersed for years in typical teacher-talk, most students need time to get used to talking with adults in a serious, respectful way. Haradon's talk is not the usual classroom banter. He doesn't work from a script or listen for specific responses. Instead he follows the logic of a student's response to the work at hand, allowing for intellectual side trips and detours that the student prompts. This does not mean that the student can talk about just anything; it means that the student can talk about the work at hand in many different ways, which inevitably means in ways that are most important to the student as well as most important to the teacher. It is hard to know where Haradon's professional approach ends and his personality begins, because he does not become a different person when he teaches. The very reason he continues to teach is that teaching expresses his personal interests and desires better than any other activity. When we can say this about most teachers, we will have solved a great many of the seemingly impossible challenges in American education today.

Teachers who wish to make things better in their schools have the greatest opportunities of all the players in modern education. What teachers do, after all, is the sum total of the education we provide our children in our schools. If teachers will fight to remain honest in their interactions with students; if they will make every class an experiment in some sound way; if they will concentrate, always, on the small battles rather than the large, they will play the decisive role in the drama to redeem our schools. Parents, politicians, citizens, and school administrators can help best by sparing no effort to support those teachers.

ADMINISTRATORS AT THEIR BEST: THE TEACHERS' ADVOCATES

School administrators—principals, superintendents, curriculum directors, and the many other central office professionals—are generally rewarded for planning and for executing plans. They take ideas, missions, and goals from a wide variety of sources (school boards, consultants, political leaders, parents) and use them to shape the way teachers teach. Occasionally these ideas come from teachers too, but no more so than from, say, state legislators. At the classroom level the "reform of the month" is generally given grudging compliance, seen more often than not as a distraction from the nuts and bolts of classroom life. Yet the best administrators are not those who wrangle the most compliance with new plans and goals. The best are those who become advocates for classroom teachers. Instead of sending the school system's messages down into the classroom, they deliver the teachers' messages up to the hierarchy.

One principal in a Texas public school describes her efforts to play this role. "I have two separate jobs as principal, as I see it. First, I run this building. I'm responsible for everything fitting together in practical terms, from the heat being on in the morning to responding to violence and creating an atmosphere that keeps the violence to a minimum. All these practical things—like serving two meals a day to eight hundred students; that's part of my job too—have not that much to do with teaching and learning. But that's what the teaching staff is for. Frankly, one-third of my teaching staff is not doing a good job, and won't do a good job. But the other two-thirds are my allies. I have no shortage of mandates from the district, from the city, from the state, and from federal programs that give us extra money. But the last thing I want to do is to go to these teachers and tell them 'do this or do that.' I'd burn out in a month. They have to understand the obligations from all the agencies that set curriculum, and then they have to be the creative force to do great things within those confines.

"We can have political conversations all day long, and plan to ignore or overthrow the standards, but what I want my teachers to answer for me is the basic question of What will you do in the classroom? If I answer that for them, they become robots. So every one of these teachers has it as his or her job to build strategies and approaches for their lessons. They can take a lot of it from the textbooks and the mandated state standards, but that's just a beginning. And some of them, really three or four out of about twenty-five, they do this across the board. A lot of the others do it with enough regularity that they contribute very important things. And then it's my job to be the communicator, to make sure that every teacher in this school knows what the others are doing. My job is to remind everyone how much freedom and professional responsibility they have, and to share the outstanding work that the other teachers are doing.

"This is a different approach than a lot of other principals in my district take, but it works very well for me, for two reasons. First, I respect these teachers as individuals, and if you tell me that it all has to come from me, that I have to outline what happens in every classroom every day, I have to ask you why all these teachers keep showing up in the morning. It can't be just to do what I'm telling them. The other reason is really a matter of self-preservation. I have no desire to run every classroom here, or even a single one. I want these teachers to run the classrooms and to surprise me with the kinds of things that I would be exhausted thinking up on my own. Look at them—twenty-five different people working, thinking, talking with these kids every day. They have the answers. I just want them to know that I'm listening, and that I'm their megaphone. Bring me the good ideas and I'll make them known, I'll tell the superintendent, I'll tell all the parents.

"You know, we have five professional development days a year when the kids all stay home and the teachers come in for training all day. Usually you get people from a college or from a textbook company to come out and do the training, or an ex-principal or someone like that, but what I do as often as I can get away with it, is I spend at least half the day with teachers in the building going over what they're doing, their best ideas, their criticisms of the textbooks and how we can work around those limitations, and it works wonderfully because they all know this is not a game, it's not about being a star or being a favorite teacher, but about how we have the same kids that we share inside this building and we have to find the best ways to get these kids through school with some positive results. I can't pay the teachers for these presentations, but I use the money I save to bring in more substitutes later in the year, and the teachers who present get more prep time later—they love that."

This principal is a risk-taker. She breaks a number of rules—rules that require her to enforce a single curriculum and teaching approach in her classrooms, rules about how in-service training days are supposed to be run—and bends an even larger number. Her trust in her teachers can backfire when a weak teacher finds his or her way onto the staff, but this principal is willing to take the risk. "Everything you do in a school involves risk," she says. "The standard model risks a kind of sterility, a regimentation of our minds and our commitments. At times my way won't work, I've seen that, but I'm betting on the power of the individuals in my classrooms over the power of the system. My small contribution is to create an environment in which teachers teach the way I taught when I was in the classroom, with a bit of independence, with a lot of support, and with the expectation that every new day is a new chance to find a new way to inspire your students. Without the chance to try new things, I don't imagine that a good teacher would want to stay in the classroom for the long haul."

Of all the risks this principal is taking, the biggest is the risk of seeming like a shirker. In general, principals are expected by their bosses to get teachers to follow instructions, in particular to get them to stick to curriculum guidelines and goals. Success is measured by students' scores on statewide tests. But as this Texas principal suggests, this kind of success offers little personal reward for an administrator who values education over test scores.

Principals who see themselves as educators first and foremost often wish they had official encouragement to spend their days differently. The best take the risks they must take in order to work as advocates for their teachers. They protect the integrity of the classroom rather than spending most of their time enforcing edicts from above. These principals become advocates for the messy, unpredictable magic of good teaching.

When we ask teachers to make their classes real, to respond to students in honest ways that not only risk but actually encourage surprises like new ideas and sudden inspirations, the teachers need support from principals and district-level administrators who actively look for and celebrate the original, unexpected achievements of good teachers. But the principals who choose not to chase the dream of higher scores, who instead choose to become advocates for their teachers, can seem to their superiors to be lying back instead of pushing forward. Where are your test-improvement programs? they might be asked. Where is your support for the new four-point plan? What, in short, are you *doing*? To respond, "I'm supporting my teachers," is risky. That might be the very best thing to do, but it does not go far in the race to *seem* busy, to demonstrate support of the new programs being implemented by a school district at a given moment. Yet the best principals take this risk. Without it their jobs would be greatly diminished.

Lew Smith, a professor of education at Fordham University and a veteran high school teacher and principal, published an article about the vital importance of taking risks shortly after the terrorist attacks on New York and Washington, D.C., on September 11, 2001. "Somehow," he wrote, "in the midst of our national school debate about standards and scores, accountability and academics, crisis management and change, a central set of questions has evaded discussion: Why do we have schools? What are they for? How might we define their purpose?" Smith argues that particularly in times of crisis, "we ought to seize the moment to ask ourselves what roles we want our schools to play." He tells two personal stories to begin answering these questions:

> I was a first-year high-school social studies teacher in an all-black school in an all-black community when the Rev. Martin Luther King Jr. was assassinated in April of 1968. Almost naively, I reported to work the day after that tragedy, a Friday, to witness emotional scenes of every stripe: disbelief, fear, shock, confusion, and rampaging rage. The questions on everyone's lips were why, how, and what does this all mean? After a weekend spent glued to the television and ripping through newspaper accounts, I had a collection of quotes and questions to share with my students on Monday. Inspired by their responses and their passion, I asked my department chair if I could change the curriculum, so that my 9th-graders could spend the remaining months of that awful spring exploring the issues surrounding Dr. King's assassination and its aftermath.
>
> More than 20 years later, I was the principal of a junior-senior high school when the Gulf War broke out. As American citizens and as educators, we were shocked and concerned and did not know what to do. But the opportunities for historical comparisons, debate of opposing viewpoints, writing personal accounts in journals, and

planning appropriate service projects were obvious. In effect, I encouraged all the teachers, of every subject and every grade, to convert their classrooms into sites of inquiry. The school, as a caring and connected community, created a wide range of academic and social vehicles to translate anger and anxiety into action.

As a teacher, Smith was more committed to the experiences and ideas of his students than he was to the curriculum he had been given. In 1968 his principal was wise to support his decision to respond to the crisis in his students' lives with an experiment in the classroom. Realize, though, that the experiment hewed closely to the mandate of a high school history class: these students were examining the nature of history itself as they wrestled with the meaning of King's death. Every question they *wanted* to ask was precisely the kind of question that makes for a serious understanding of history. How and why was King killed? Whose interests did the killing serve? What is the proper role of the individual citizen in the wake of the killing? By responding to his students as individuals with passions, ideas, and feelings, Smith clearly engaged their minds more powerfully than the standard curriculum could have. By taking the risk of deviating from a planned and approved curriculum, Smith taught his students more, and better.

Decades later, as a principal, Smith's greatest act was to recall the classroom teacher he had once been. He did not impose a top-down approach to the Gulf War on his teachers. Instead he encouraged them to experiment with their own approaches, to engage their students' responses to the world-historical events unfolding before them. He understood that as a principal he could make a great contribution to his teachers and his students by presenting the teachers with a *challenge* to plan, rather than with a plan; with a question, rather than with an answer. Why? Because students bring to school an almost infinite amount of intellectual energy. If their teachers interact with them honestly and respectfully, and if they constantly seek new ways to unlock that intellectual energy, more of it will be loosed in the classroom. If teachers try instead to follow a fixed plan, to move from one preconceived instructional point to the next with little regard for the potential of students to reveal or invent challenging ideas, a great opportunity is lost.

Former Arizona State Superintendent of Education Lisa Graham Keegan reflected the same spirit when she shared this story: "I'll ask my seven-year-old what she's going to do for a living, and her response is different every day. She'll come into my room and say, 'Mom, I could be so many things.' Those are the best days for a parent. My job as superintendent is to create that possibility and that mindset for any child."

That celebration of the unexpected, that faith in the open-ended imagination of students, is too rare among school administrators today, whose success is measured in too many cases by the fluctuations of test scores in their schools and districts. Graham Keegan is suggesting another path, and a good one.

Roy Romer, the former governor of Colorado and current superintendent of schools in Los Angeles, makes a similar point in different terms. "In education there are three things that are important," Romer says. "They are instruction, instruction, instruction." Romer's words convey a great deal. He pointedly does not include in his ringing recitation of priorities words like "out-comes," "measurement," or "accountability," the most vivid fighting words in today's schools. Instead he quietly makes the point that testing is a mere appendage to what is tested: learning. And learning, going back to the ancient definition, is all about the interaction between a student and a teacher, not a student and a test, nor a student and a "standard."

The scholar Alfie Kohn makes a more direct attack on the testing movement: "Standardized testing," Kohn writes, "has swelled and mutated, like a creature in one of those old horror movies, to the point that it now threatens to swallow our schools whole." Kohn and the many other opponents to the swelling emphasis on standardized tests address what is lost in districts that have made higher scores the highest good in their work. It is true that where test scores go up, administrators are generally applauded; where they do not go up, administrators are often fired. School leaders who wish to do more—particularly those who wish to tap the power of their teachers in order to breathe new life into Romer's three critical tasks—too often must become resisters of, even rebels against, an easy status quo that mistakenly presumes testing to be simple, honest, and effective in measuring the success of our schools. The choice here is not between embracing or rejecting the value of standardized tests. Rather, it is a question of whether the higher test scores are seen as a good in themselves (not a wise view), or as a reflection and validation of other things, like better instruction, as Romer suggests, that teachers drive and school leaders support.

Another way to frame this distinction is to look at whether a particular district embraces a push for higher scores in the short run or in the long run. Many tricks can be used to pump up scores in the short run, a good number of them worthless distractions from real education. In fact, in some cases higher test scores can be a bad thing, because they represent the triumph of short-term thinking over long-term thinking. Improving scores in the long run is clearly the greater good that results from teachers teaching better, let loose by their administrators to experiment, to innovate, and to demand difficult, thoughtful work from their students.

A remarkable example of higher test scores that, from an educational perspective, represent a kind of bad news comes in the story of a Florida elementary school that went from an overall test-score-based rating of F, for failure, to an A. Doing well on the standardized tests in Florida became the overriding theme of the school for months before the exam date in 2001. The preceding year the superintendent had said to the teachers and administrators at the school with the F rating, "The bottom line is that your job is on the line."

Education Week reported that "the F grade triggered visits from state education officials, school district personnel, and staff members from other Florida districts. State law requires the Florida education department to provide help to schools that earn a failing grade." This was top-down school reform without a doubt: triggered by statewide tests, replete with state and district-level plans, guidelines, staff, and threats. Many good things resulted: more money flowed into the school from funds earmarked for schools at risk of being shut down; more teachers and teachers' assistants were hired; and the average class size in the school shrank. But test-prep thinking took over the school completely. Reading teachers adopted the strategy of having students read only state-test-sized passages instead of whole stories or books, always accompanied by practice exam questions. And they taught the students to read the test questions about the passages before the passages themselves. "Why do we read the questions first?" one teacher asked her class. A student responded, "So we can understand and get the right answer." The teacher beamed—that was the answer she was looking for. No teacher who values the power of literature would endorse this as the best approach for learning, but it turned out to be the best approach for passing the state tests.

A few days before the big test, called the FCAT in Florida, a school assembly was scheduled for a pep rally. Students wore T-shirts with slogans about beating the FCATs. A teacher dressed up in a cat outfit and roamed around trying to scare students, who were prompted to brush off the test-cat with brave gestures. The next day the assistant principal announced over the school-wide PA system, "A ferocious animal is coming. But we are not afraid." At the close of the announcement, she added, "Do anything it takes to be winners." Most educators would bridle at that notion—do anything it takes to win. Is that, finally, the lesson we want our schools to teach? Is that a reasonable approach to test-taking in our schools?

Much can be gained by looking at test scores and taking them seriously, but in too many American schools today education itself is being displaced by a kind of test mania. Robert Maynard Hutchins, president of the University of Chicago for many years, often remarked that his personal form of heresy was to believe that the purpose of education was, in fact, education. In his particular circumstances, he was talking about valuing education above sports and money on the college campus. Among American schools, we must say today that the purpose of our schools is education, not test scores. Test scores are useful tools to measure the education we fill our schools with, but they do great harm if they displace that education with ideas like winning at any cost.

And so, first among the "do's" for administrators who wish to make important and lasting change in their school is to resist the assumption that test scores are the best indicator of success. People who work outside the world of educational administration may underestimate the courage this requires. In most school districts today, raising test scores is seen as the fundamental duty of administrators, at almost any cost. Recall the example of the Chicago school that saw its student population change dramatically over a few years, from the children of largely uneducated Central American immigrants to the children of well-educated European refugees. Test scores went up markedly, but they would have risen even had the students been barred from instruction and merely required to show up for exam day. This story should demand at least a degree of skepticism toward the testing movement.

The second "do" for administrators is to view their roles as bottom-up advocates for teachers, with the special responsibility to cultivate, recognize, and communicate new ideas that germinate in the classroom. Administrators must also play a vital role in evaluating teachers. Notice how the two principals we've heard from in this book who run programs to elicit and communicate new ideas from teachers mention that a good number of teachers choose not to participate. These principals are able to evaluate their staff with real insight because they are on the prowl for original ideas. They give whatever official support they can to teachers who take risks in order to innovate, and they give these teachers a great deal of unofficial support.

A POSITIVE ROLE FOR POLITICIANS
AND POLICYMAKERS

Politicians and high-level policymakers tend to make teachers and principals nervous. Particularly because of the tough curriculum and testing standards issuing from state legislatures and the U.S. Department of Education in the last decade, many teachers expect little good to come from elected officials. Stories like Dennis Littky's in New Hampshire add little to inspire confidence. Yet state legislators do have a vital role to play in aiding classroom teachers and in raising standards at state teachers' colleges.

Few people who spend much time in the education departments of American colleges and universities are very happy with them. Elite colleges often do not offer education majors at all. Instead they encourage students who wish to teach to major in a traditional academic subject—history, biology, etc.—and then to build on that firm knowledge with additional coursework after graduation. (Harvard and Columbia both house graduate schools of education known to be among the best in the world, but neither offers an undergraduate major.) On those campuses that do offer undergraduate education majors, average scores for education majors on college entrance tests are generally lower than those of other students. Their overall grade point averages tend to be lower too. The good news is that the past ten years have seen considerable improvement in education programs on college campuses, largely in response to growing public awareness of just how bad so many education programs had become.

The problems in most college education programs begin with how education professors are trained and evaluated. Excellent teaching is not enough to earn and keep a faculty position in the typical education department. Research is an important part of the professional package. But what exactly is "research" in the field of education? In some cases it's straightforward: many education professors conduct research in such matters as how students from different economic and ethnic backgrounds perform in a range of subjects, or how their families view education. But most education research is interpretive, proposing to reveal through experiment or the development of new theories the right direction for teachers to take on any number of issues, and this interpretive research can't help but stray from the realities of the K-12 classroom. The pressure on professors to publish articles and present research papers only pushes professors further away from the culture of the schoolteacher, and toward the distinct culture of the education professoriat. And so professors of education spend a great deal of time researching, writing, and presenting papers with titles like "Guided Verbalization for Conceptual Understanding: A Scaffold for Making Sense of Multiple Traces of Cognition" and "Developing the Third Eye: Applying Personality and Multicultural Social Reconstructionism to Action Research." (These two papers were presented at the American Educational Research Association conference in 2002, the primary national conference for education professors.) No doubt the professors who researched these papers could make a case for their relevance to teachers in ordinary school classrooms. But would we even want them to?

Even when professors conduct research that sounds friendlier to ordinary teachers, leading to papers like "Becoming a Member: Welcoming Young Children into Communities of Literacy," also presented at the 2002 AERA conference, the research suffers from profound limitations. At its best, education research can tell you that if you try a certain method under certain circumstances, you can achieve a predictable result. If that result is a good one, you'll want to try the method—if you can duplicate the circumstances, which is extraordinarily difficult.

At one extreme, educational research can be made reliable by isolating the issue being studied from other variables. For example, if we want to test whether a certain approach to teaching reading works better than another approach, we need to create an environment in which all other variables—teachers quitting, students changing schools, episodes of school violence, changing school schedules—are kept perfectly steady for a long enough time so that we can see how the new approach helps or hurts. But no teacher will be able to keep those variables steady in the real world. So how valuable is that research after all, if real-world teachers can't duplicate the conditions in which we know the new teaching approach works?

On the other hand, we can try out the new reading methodology in a series of real schools. But the results will be less consistent because of the impact of uncontrolled variables. In one test school, for example, a school shooting incident might disrupt instruction and frighten students for weeks or months. Certainly they won't learn what they otherwise would have learned, and no matter how good the new program, it will probably show poor re-sults while the school recovers. In other schools, some of the teachers trained in the new program might be transferred out un-expectedly, or fall ill. Replacement teachers will probably not do justice to the experimental program, and the outcome will be weaker than it otherwise might have been. Of course, in some of the other schools the expected results might indeed emerge. But what else might have been going on in those schools during the research period? New school uniforms made mandatory, perhaps? A long school day put in place? Lunch period rescheduled, so now the students are not as hungry during their reading period? How can we say that the results we see are a function of our new reading program and none of these other real-world variables?

This is the muddled world of education research, and the large majority of college and university education programs have research at their heart. But not all. A number of outstanding pro-grams pay relatively little attention to education research and are better for it. The Bank Street College of Education and the Univer-sity of Illinois at Chicago (UIC) are among those that have found ways to guide their students toward an understanding of educa-tion that is rigorous, creative, and grounded in the realities of the classroom, without an excessive emphasis on the publish-or-perish ethos of professional professoring. Instead of reputations for top-quality research articles, these schools enjoy reputations for producing top-quality teachers, a distinction to be proud of.

As a teacher at a number of colleges, I've gotten used to the sad fact that education majors tend to be the weaker students in most courses. But not at UIC. My first clue that something differ-ent was happening in the education school at UIC came when I

taught a literature course there. To my surprise, the English education majors in the course began to dominate the class. As a
group they were more articulate and knew more than the rest of
the class. That made me curious about what UIC was doing right
that most other education colleges were not.

UIC is the classic urban public college. Its campus architec-
ture holds all the warmth of a state prison. The few bits of green
are generally speckled with refuse and battered by Chicago's
winds. The one spot that students occasionally take over for Fris-
bee games is sandwiched between a busy boulevard and an inter-
state highway. Most students live off-campus, and most hold jobs.
Many are the first in their families to attend college. This is precisely the kind of college that trains most of America's teachers—
a no-frills public institution that has more in common with
working-class neighborhoods than with Ivy League campuses. So
how does UIC turn out education majors who perform so well?

The secret lies in the education division's tough admissions
standards. At most public colleges, choosing to major in education isn't much harder than checking a box on the enrollment
forms. At UIC, gaining full standing as an education major takes
two years, and many who plan to major in education don't make
the cut. First, students must earn a grade point average of 3.5 in
their two years of initial coursework across the university. They
must complete sixty hours of pre-major coursework in the education department, and pass at least one college math course. Every
aspiring education major must also spend one hundred hours in
supervised work with children—and all one hundred hours must
be taken in a single institution (students can't put in ten hours
here and ten there). Then they must submit a writing sample and

pass an impromptu writing exam. Finally, every applicant must have a successful interview with an education faculty member.

These standards ensure that applicants understand what working with children is like. They also ensure that education majors are academically capable, that they can communicate well, and that they understand what the world of schools in the United States is like. Most of the faculty research that UIC does encourage draws students into local schools, to help build and sustain classroom-level experiments. This is research less about big ideas and long-term studies than about trying to make demonstration projects based on simple observations, like the UIC Small Schools Project, which builds off the idea that small schools generally work better than large schools. Students are encouraged—and often required—to work alongside their professors and local teachers in these experiments, gaining a ground-level view of how ideas that make lasting change can emerge in the classroom.

Perhaps the most important effect of the tough academic standards and the exemplary research projects at UIC is the great respect for the study of education across the campus. This seems to funnel the best students toward the education school. At the college I attended, the State University of New York at Binghamton, every once in a while I would find myself sharing a meal with students who wished to major in business. They often talked about the tough requirements for admission to the business school, and everyone took for granted that however we felt about business as an academic subject—personally, I shared the antipathies of my fellow English and philosophy majors—business students were a bright and hardworking bunch who deserved respect. Many students who arrived at college unsure of what to study headed for the business school because they wanted to work hard and reach the highest goals they could achieve on campus. UIC's great achievement is to create a path of aspiration and accomplishment on its own campus that attracts the best and brightest students to education. That's a model that other colleges, and our society at large, would do well to emulate.

Teacher education programs in Massachusetts illustrate the point well. Every year the state monitors the percentage of students graduating from each college education program who pass the state teacher-certification exam. Schools that fall below 80 percent risk being shut down by the state. On the whole, colleges that have higher admissions standards and smaller education programs see a greater percentage of their graduates pass the exam— no great surprise there. College of Holy Cross, a highly selective private college with about a dozen education graduates each year, often sees all of its graduates pass the exam. Fitchburg State College, on the other hand, has a program ten times the size of the Holy Cross program, and with decidedly low admission standards. In the year 2000, Fitchburg State saw only 62 percent of its graduates pass.

What are we to make of this data? Certainly we can't insist that schools hire only graduates of small, elite colleges to become teachers. But we can look to the schools like UIC that open their doors to students with a broad range of academic backgrounds, and draw the best of them into an engaging and effective education program. In Massachusetts, 88 percent of the education graduates from the University of Massachusetts at Amherst, the state's flagship campus with fairly high standards, passed the state exam in 2000. At the University of Massachusetts campus in Boston, with somewhat lower admissions standards, only 80 percent did. At Framingham State College, general admissions standards are lower than those at UMass Boston, and comparable to the standards at Fitchburg State, where only 62 percent of the education graduates passed the state test. But at Framingham, 86 percent of the graduates passed. What was Framingham doing right that other schools should emulate?

The answer comes in two parts. First, Framingham has a strong emphasis on what it calls "coordinate education majors," and on joint degrees. A smaller proportion of Framingham State education majors get a degree in education alone. More commonly, students do education degrees jointly with subject departments, and get "coordinate" degrees in those subjects as well. Many take the full load of courses to earn full degrees in English as well as full degrees in other subjects. Just as important, though, Framingham does not allow students to be fully accepted as education majors until they have passed the reading and writing component of the state certification test. The test is not terribly difficult,* but as many as 20 percent of test takers fail it each year. By requiring that students pass this test before they take many of

*A sample question, prepared by Wheelock College to help its students prepare for the test, is based on a reading passage from 1933, about the town of Salem, Massachusetts. This is part of the reading passage: "We think little of the use of the deep estuaries about Salem Bay as a means of transportation, but when the roads were little more than bridle paths, it meant much to be able to haul farm produce a few miles to a landing and then transport it the last six or seven miles by water to Salem. Even boating produce down Plum Island Sound and around Cape Ann was easier than hauling it ten or fifteen miles overland." This is the test question based on this passage: What is the writer's main idea in paragraph 2 ("We think little . . . ten or fifteen miles overland")? The choices:

the more advanced education courses at the college, and before they become full majors in the education program, Framingham raises the intellectual level of its advanced courses (which means that the teachers created by those courses will know a little more and be able to think at a higher level), creates the impression that the education major is a distinction that must be earned (which will attract better students to the education major), and chooses not to deliver to America's classrooms teachers who cannot read and write well. The Framingham program is not as stringent as UIC's, and the teachers it creates are not, as a group, as exemplary. But they are a step above the graduates from some of Framingham's peer education colleges, and they demonstrate an interim step taken in the transition from a typically weak education college to an outstanding one.

Bank Street College of Education is already outstanding, though in some ways it is the very opposite of UIC and Framingham State. Bank Street is a small private school with a focus on graduate education. Bank Street follows a particular philosophy of child-centered and project-based learning, building very much on the ideas of John Dewey. But more important than the theory of child-centered education is the fact that Bank Street's building—

---

a. We tend to forget about means of transportation.

b. The easily navigable bay at Salem helped to facilitate the selling of agricultural products for surrounding farms.

c. Boating produce down Plum Island Sound and around Cape Ann was easier than hauling ten or fifteen miles overland.

d. Transportation by water was easier than transportation by land in the seventeenth century.

The correct answer is (b).

no longer on Bank Street but miles uptown in New York City, on the edge of Harlem—houses a school for children itself as large as the graduate school for educators. Children are everywhere at Bank Street. They share a cafeteria with the college students, they bump them in the hallways, and their presence is the one unavoidable fact of everyday life at the school.

That presence reflects the core values of Bank Street College, powerfully articulated in 1916 by the school's founder, Lucy Sprague Mitchell, in "A Credo for Bank Street":

What potentialities in human beings—children, teachers, and ourselves—do we want to see develop?

- A zest for living that comes from taking in the world with all five senses alert.
- Lively intellectual curiosities that turn the world into an exciting laboratory and keep one ever a learner.
- Flexibility when confronted with change and ability to relinquish patterns that no longer fit the present.
- The courage to work, unafraid and efficiently, in a world of new needs, new problems, and new ideas.
- Gentleness combined with justice in passing judgments on other human beings.
- Sensitivity, not only to the external formal rights of the "other fellow," but to him as another human being seeking a good life through his own standards.
- A striving to live democratically, in and out of schools, as the best way to advance our concept of democracy.
- Our credo demands ethical standards as well as scientific attitudes. Our work is based on the faith

that human beings can improve the society they have created.

The language of this credo—words like "faith," "justice," "democracy," and "courage"—is almost impossible to find in the documents that describe other education colleges. Bank Street succeeds so well with its students in large part because it continues to teach the values that these words suggest. It continues to teach teachers to experiment, to find better alternatives to school orthodoxies, and to become forces for positive change in the lives of the teachers, students, and schools they will know as educators. Most education colleges teach students what they need to know to adapt to an educational system that does a great deal wrong. Bank Street teaches a different lesson: insist on high standards and real compassion for your students, and make the system adapt to you. That's a radical concept that has produced great results since the school was founded early in the twentieth century.

Like UIC, Bank Street also puts education students into closer contact with professors than most other education schools do. Students spend much of their time in "advisement," a tutorial system similar to the British model of university education. Professors tailor assignments to individual students, and students present their ongoing work to professors one-on-one in regular private meetings. Students can't sit at the back of lecture halls and doze off. They can't skate through with borderline grades and get their degrees and certifications anyway. Their professors develop a finely calibrated sense of what each student is learning, and instruction proceeds more on the basis of what students are actually learning than on the basis of what professors thought they might learn when they originally planned their lectures.

Must the study of education in our colleges remain undistinguished? Must it feed a culture of mediocrity in the schools? Of course not. Model programs, like those of UIC and Bank Street, are not hard to find. They are, alas, hard to replicate. They require that education colleges replace large lecture halls, abstract research, and multiple-choice exams with high expectations and individual attention for education majors. Not very different, after all, from what K-12 schools ought to be offering their own students.

State legislators in Massachusetts have set important standards for their education colleges, and those standards have led to a wave of examination and improvement in these colleges. Framingham State's success is a direct result of those standards, and UIC could not have achieved all it has in its education program without support from the state legislators of Illinois. Schools like Bank Street will always represent models of excellence worth emulating. But the lion's share of our nation's teachers will continue to study at public colleges. Any legislator who works to preserve, honor, and improve those institutions does more good than he could with any number of high-profile tours of local grade schools and stump speeches about test scores.

THE ROLE OF PARENTS

Parental involvement in schools takes two forms. First, parents need to support their children's learning at home. This is perhaps the more important of the two kinds of involvement, and one that reaches beyond the individual. If every parent were to provide effective at-home support for learning, our schools would be better, because most students would perform at higher levels, have fewer behavior problems, and be prepared to participate in more challenging intellectual work at school. The research on at-home support for learning presents an overwhelming consensus: students do significantly better at school when their parents talk to them about their schoolwork every day; students whose parents read books regularly for their own interest and alongside their children do better at school; and students whose parents know the names of their teachers and know what topics they are studying in their classes do better at school.

In too many cases, parents are not doing what they might. Lawrence Steinberg's research, collected in the book *Beyond the Classroom*, concludes that in the United States, 20 percent of parents have no connection at all to their child's educational life. They don't know what they're studying, who their teachers are, or whether they are even attending school. Only one in five parents attends school programs regularly, and only 40 percent attend at all. One-third of the students say their parents have no idea of whether they are doing well or poorly in school, and only a third of students say their parents spend any time talking to them—about anything—each day.

Clearly, the first step for parents who want to improve schools is to spend time with their own children, reading and talking about what they read, getting to know the assigned work in every class, and being sure to keep a dialogue about school, education, and ideas alive in the home.

The second kind of parent involvement begins when a parent

ventures into the school building itself. Most parents who volunteer at schools have an experience something like this: Their children start at new schools, or for some other reason they are inspired to become involved in a school that their child has already been attending for a while. Perhaps they have concerns about the school, perhaps there's been a change in personal commitments that has made time available, or perhaps for no reason at all—it just feels like time to get involved. So the typical parent asks another parent at the school how to get involved, and that parent shares a personal experience. It might run something like this: "The debate team is the best thing going, and they need your help," or "We're doing a big fund drive, and you'll be a great addition to the team." Of course, it could run more like this: "Well, it's only a certain crowd that's really involved, and they're not my kind of people." Instead of asking friends, some parents will march right into the school office and say to whoever is sitting at the main desk, "I want to volunteer; what can I do?" Others will talk to their child's teachers and ask how they can help. In too many cases, though, interested parents will be channeled into official, school-wide parent volunteer programs, often involving fund-raising, program development, or the running of events, and this presents a special challenge.

The greatest strength of these programs—that they are centrally organized and coordinated with the many support, enrichment, and improvement programs in schools—is also their greatest weakness. Programs created by school administrations are always likely to support the administrations' needs and goals, and to reflect the view of a given school from the administration's perspective. But just as the most effective school reform efforts begin at the classroom level, parent involvement also does its greatest good at the level of the individual classroom rather than at the institutional level. Many parent involvement programs are structured to create a bond between the parent and the school. Far better to create a bond between the parent and the teacher, or the teacher and the classroom.

Schools are institutions; their function is to organize, regulate, and aggregate. The function of the teacher is often the opposite: to empower the individual student, to inspire unexpected new ideas, and, as the writer Earl Shorris describes his own efforts to bring classical education to housing projects and Indian reservations, "to make people dangerous"—to help them become literate, informed, and articulate to the point that they take up the American challenge continually to reshape and reform our institutions. So there is a positive tension here between the institution—the school—as it is today, and the school as it might be remade by the very students it educates. The school today gives its students the tools they need to change that school, to criticize and refigure the very goals and methods of the school itself, so that tomorrow the school will be different, and better.

Schools are created by a society at large, to fulfill the broad cultural aim of educating young people. At the highest level, schools do the work of a whole culture. At the institutional level, though, schools develop their own institutional needs, their own politics, their own habits. School administrators too easily value the needs of the institution—smooth day-to-day functioning, stability and predictability—over both the broader need of the culture (to educate young people) and the need of the classroom. The individual teacher's vivid contact with individual students has much in common with the highest goals of education; it is the institutional force, the inertia of an organization with a building, a payroll, a social structure all of its own, that is foreign. This split is real but often ignored by parents who wish to help improve schools. These parents must choose, and to make their greatest contribution they must choose to serve the interests of the students and their teachers instead of—often in subtle opposition to—the interests of the institutions that house them.

The three "do's" for teachers and administrators who want to make a difference—emphasize individuals, keep it real, and make it new—apply to parents too. Parent volunteer programs that reflect these principles can be a wonderful tool for parents.

If the parent's challenge begins with building the right kind of relationship with the teacher, that relationship begins with the question, "How can I help you?" Some teachers will answer that question in practical ways that reflect their practical challenges ("Can you stop by to watch the class for ten minutes at about eleven, so I can use the bathroom?"). Others will answer with a year-long strategy in mind ("Can you help to organize the other parents in the class to raise money for special projects?"). The best overall goal for a parent is to help the teacher teach better. Raising money for trips is a fine thing, but if the teacher does not help students learn from what they see outside the classroom, so much is lost.

In a few schools, parents have the remarkable opportunity to help select teachers—the kind of higher-level, out-of-the-classroom volunteering that makes a tremendous difference because it so directly affects the classroom. Kentucky enacted a school reform program in 1998 that mandates school councils in some schools, made up of parents, teachers, and administrators. These councils often do the actual hiring of new teachers. As one Kentucky principal says, "When parents participate in interviews for school personnel, they ask, 'Is this the type of person I want my child to spend time with every day? Do they like kids? Would my child enjoy having this person as a teacher?'" A parent volunteer in this principal's school notes that since becoming involved in the school council, "I haven't been asked to bake a single cookie."

This is perhaps the highest praise a parent can give to a school's parent volunteer program. Cookies are wonderful, but they are far from the real business of schools. Schools that protect their own institutional habits and interests try to keep parents away from the real educational work they do, so they push cookie baking and other fund-raising activities. Schools that look for ways to support teachers in their classrooms help parents find ways to help directly in those classrooms, to give them the chance to do some real good.

THE ROLE OF THE CITIZEN

Parents are not alone in wanting to help make our schools better. Every citizen has a duty to work toward schools worthy of our children. Acting on that duty requires some general understanding of how good a job our teachers are doing. Unfortunately, many of the "standardized" tests that are used in teacher certification programs are better suited to evaluating groups than individuals. That is, if you compare the test scores of all graduates of a teacher training program to all the graduates from another school's teacher training program, you'll learn a lot about the student bodies of these schools *in aggregate*. If you compare all the scores from mid-career teachers taking an exam for recertification from one district to those in another, you'll learn a lot about how those districts compare to each other. Just as looking at the average SAT scores of newly admitted students can help you get a sense of what a specific college is like, looking at test scores on teacher exams can help a skillful observer understand the overall abilities of teachers in a given state, town, or even in a given school.

But at the level of the individual, these tests tell us less than we often think. Measuring an individual requires—and this should come as no surprise—*individual* effort and attention. If you want to move to a new school district, looking at the average score of the district's teachers on standardized tests is probably a good idea. If you're choosing a graduate program to attend, looking at the students' average test scores will reveal a great deal about the school and its student body as a group. But if you want to choose the best teacher for your child, you need to meet that teacher and spend a fair amount of time taking his or her measure.

One of the great success stories in educational reform in the United States in recent years has nothing to do with the structures and systems of schools, and everything to do with individual attention to individual teachers. In 1987 the National Board for Professional Teacher Standards, a private group supported by federal education funds, began inviting teachers to apply for National Board Certification in their disciplines. To date more than seventeen thousand teachers have become certified through the program, and they are widely recognized as among the very best in the profession.

National Board Certification requires two levels of examination. One resembles traditional standardized testing and involves a series of exams on one's knowledge of education and teaching in general, and in subject areas like math, biology, and English. The other is more subjective and takes several months. Teachers put together a portfolio of their own work in the classroom (on paper, on video, and on-line), their students' work, and their colleagues' assessments of their achievements. The entire process is expensive (typical costs for teachers are close to $2,500) and time-consuming (some districts offer release time from teaching while teachers work on their applications). Hundreds of school districts and several states actually increase the pay of teachers who achieve National Board Certification, as a reward; some actually pay the fees and expenses for their teachers.

But some districts oppose National Board Certification. Critics say that the program has produced little evidence that students benefit from their teachers holding national certification, and that the program sets its own goals without regard to district-level plans and goals. The *Rocky Mountain News*, published in Denver, recently opposed state support for teachers seeking National Board Certification, echoing other critics of the Board by saying that the program was "unproven." But in 2000 the National Board funded a research study of National Board Certified teachers and their students at the University of North Carolina. In this straightforward, quantitative research project, the results were clear. "In every comparison between NBCTs [National Board

Certified Teachers] and non-NBCTs on the dimensions of teaching excellence," the final research report said,

> NBCTs obtained higher mean scores. In 11 of the 13 comparisons, the differences were highly statistically significant. In eight of the comparisons, differences between the two groups held up against what is generally regarded as the most stringent statistical test available. The conclusion seems clear: the National Board Certified Teachers in this sample possess, to a considerably greater degree than non-certified teachers, those characteristics of expert teaching that have emerged from the body of research on teaching and learning.

Put more simply, the report says that National Board Certified teachers are, on the whole, better teachers than the average teacher without national certification. R. Gerald Longo, superintendent of schools in Pennsylvania's Quaker Valley School District, tried unsuccessfully to get state support for putting a number of his teachers through the National Board Certification process, based upon a simple observation: "Everyone who has ever been to school knows that good teachers are central to good schools. The money spent by policymakers on gimmicks would be better used to encourage teachers to seek this credential and to reach for the apex of their profession."

President Bush has spoken often about testing teachers to be sure they meet reasonable standards of knowledge and ability. At Eden Prairie High School in Minnesota in 2002, he said, "Teachers want their profession to have the highest of high standards. . . . If we want to have a teaching profession that is held in high regard, we must have confidence in the teachers' colleges and those coming into the teacher ranks that they can do the job expected of them. We owe it to the parents. And, most of all, we owe it to the students." Few would disagree. But most of the funding for teacher testing in Bush's Department of Education is going into standardized exams. These exams fit with the system-level view of schools that sees teachers in the aggregate. The more difficult task of approaching, evaluating, and inspiring teachers as individuals costs more but delivers far better and more sustainable results. President Bush has won the debate over whether teachers should be tested. Now that the debate is over, the more important question of *how* to evaluate teachers stands before us. The National Board has offered the most inspiring answer to date and deserves the support of anyone interested in creating and supporting an elite group of teachers throughout the nation.

That support will come from many quarters. Interestingly, though the National Board is supported by the National Education Association and most of its local chapters (many actually include increased pay for nationally certified teachers as a demand in contract negotiations), plenty of teachers oppose the whole idea of national certification. This opposition reflects the unfortunate habits of many teachers to view any kind of competition as unfair and any kind of elitism as harmful to all teachers. Ambition itself becomes a dirty word among some teachers, and that is a shame.

In some ways, teaching in the United States today is itself a monkish pursuit. It is not a job for those who wish to make a lot of money, not a job for those who want power, and not a job for those who want to pick up the newspaper and see their picture on the front page. It *is* a job, we often say, for people who want to make a difference. But it is also a job for people who hope to accomplish difficult things. It is a job for people who want to see their work have an impact on hundreds and thousands of lives. For those who do it exceedingly well, teaching *is* about power. These teachers reach generations into the future, touching the children and grandchildren of their students by teaching them well. To be among the very best at that work is an ambition we should seek to inspire, and celebrate. Becoming that good a teacher—the kind of teacher students remember for decades, the kind who can reach all kinds of students in all kinds of ways—requires talent *and* ambition. We ought to do everything we can to fire up those ambitions and put them to work in the service of our nation's children.

At the beginning of this book I mentioned the Hippocratic Oath that physicians swear to, beginning with the promise to "First, do no harm." While schools in general would do well to follow this principle, ordinary citizens who wish to help schools need this lesson more than most. Good teachers spend all day working to improve their classrooms; good school administrators spend much of their time attracting and supporting the best teachers they can find; involved parents help schools most when they offer practical aid to individual teachers; and the rest of us make the greatest contributions to improving our schools not when we suggest answers to our schools' problems, but when we address the right questions to the right people. Specifically, we do our best when we face a talented teacher and ask, How can we help?

7

Everyone's Work

Every American has a large stake in the quality of our nation's schools. Good education brings more thoughtful, capable citizens into the public sphere, and it brings more depth to the private lives we share with the people we care about most. No one wins when schools are weak; we all benefit when they are strong. As Plato wrote more than two thousand years ago, the reform of our nation's schools is the work of every man and every woman. Indeed, we have no shortage of pundits, politicians, and public notables loudly engaged in school reform today. Elected officials have a great deal to say about fixing schools. Business people generally have a good number of ideas to improve schools too. Seldom, though, are teachers offered the opportunity to join in the public debate.

Andy Baumgartner teaches kindergarten in Georgia and in 2000 was named National Teacher of the Year by the U.S. Department of Education. His experience that year led him to write about the role of teachers in the national school reform debate: "As National Teacher of the Year," he wrote in a column for the National Education Association, the largest of the teachers' unions,

> you receive standing ovations before uttering a word, because you represent all of America's classroom teachers. Total strangers come up to you and thank you for the contributions of an entire profession. It's been one heartwarming affirmation after another for teachers.
>
> Until you speak out about educational policy, that is.
>
> Then you encounter the great paradox. Americans value, even revere teachers—I can attest to that. But when the discussion turns to how to improve education, politicians relegate teachers to the back of the class.
>
> My home state of Georgia, for example, had a 66-person commission on school reform, but, amazingly, less than 5 percent of them were practicing teachers. . . . When I used a recognition ceremony in the Georgia State Senate to express my disagreement with the commission's recommendations, especially those that would undermine the teaching profession, I apparently crossed some line meant to keep teachers in their place.
>
> In short order I was uninvited to speak to the Georgia House of Representatives. The governor failed to show up for a scheduled photo session. . . . And a state representative from my area publicly apologized for my words and publicly criticized the impropriety of my making a "political statement" in the Georgia Senate, of all places.

Baumgartner wants to see schools improved, but his twenty years in the classroom and his one year on the national political circuit as Teacher of the Year have turned him off to the big ideas of reform, and led him back to the classroom. "Respect is the key word here," he says of school reform. "Show me a school system that truly respects teachers, and I will show you a school system that's doing right by its students."

Suggested Reading

BEFORE the twentieth century, Horace Mann was by far the most influential educator in the United States. His short 1838 book *The Republic and the School* is a declaration of war against typical schooling in the United States at the time. Mann makes his case against the low standards and disorganized teachings of locally supported one-room schoolhouses. He argues instead for the establishment of regular grade levels (first grade, second grade, and so on) based on students' ages, and for a common, secular national curriculum for all American schools. Mann won his battle, and his impact on American schools continues to be enormous. *The Republic and the School* is a kind of prehistory of the schools we have today and explains a great deal of how they got to be the way they are.

John Dewey's *School and Society*, published in 1900, represented the first concerted resistance to Mann's model of schooling. Dewey argues that the regimentation and regularization of the

205

classroom that Mann put into place create an undemocratic spirit in schools, and turn children off to the real pleasures of learning. His alternative emphasizes project-based learning and respectful collaboration among teachers and students. "School," Dewey writes, "is not preparation for life, but life itself." Dewey's book *Experience and Education*, published in 1938, offers a more detailed discussion of the same beliefs but with a number of interesting concessions based on almost forty years of classroom experimentation in the intervening years.

W. E. B. Du Bois, the first African American to receive a Ph.D. from Harvard—an accomplishment made necessary only because Du Bois ran out of funds to support his doctoral studies at the more prestigious University of Berlin—published *The Souls of Black Folk* in 1903 and included in that slim volume the essay "The Talented Tenth." There he argues for a serious commitment to education in the humanities for black Americans, in direct contrast to Booker T. Washington's call for vocational training only for African Americans in his 1901 autobiography, *Up from Slavery*. The Du Bois/Washington conflict echoes the Dewey/Mann argument and anticipates the debates over humanities education for poor students that continue today, particularly in the work of Robert Maynard Hutchins and, more recently, Earl Shorris in his 2001 book *Riches for the Poor*. Jane Addams, the founder of Hull House in Chicago, made a similar case for high academic standards combined with firmly democratic aspirations for all students in her 1902 book *Democracy and Social Ethics*, though this work is often overlooked by students of the history of American education.

Hutchins, the president of the University of Chicago and the founder, with Mortimer Adler, of the Great Books Foundation, collected a number of his speeches on education in the 1943 book *Education for Freedom*. His main argument recurs in many of those speeches: "The purpose of education," he wrote, "is education"—not football, not career preparation, and not the development of social skills suited for factory-style social regimentation. Hutchins strongly believed that most classrooms at every level of education in the United States included too little serious study of important ideas and too little serious dialogue. Both conservative—he believed that only the Western classics were worth taking seriously—and radical in his respect for the capabilities of the individual student, Hutchins often found himself in conflict with Dewey, though most students of education who read both men today find a great deal of common ground.

The writings of James Herndon, a junior high school teacher, represented a new wave of education criticism very different from the serious and elevated prose of Mann, Dewey, Addams, and Hutchins. Herndon's breakout book, *The Way It 'Spozed to Be*, published in 1968, warmly tells the story of his class of rowdy students in the rough-and-tumble school he finds himself assigned to as a new teacher. As much a study of the hearts and minds of these students as a polemic about education policy, *The Way It 'Spozed to Be* affirmed the dignity and intelligence of low-performing students and, along with Jonathan Kozol's *Death at an Early Age* and Herbert Kohl's *35 Children*, both published in 1967, helped create the new genre of the radical teaching memoir. Pat Conroy's 1972 book *The Water Is Wide*, the basis for the popular movie *Conrack*, followed their lead, as did Philip Lopate's 1975 *Being with Children*, Richard Meisler's 1984 *Trying Freedom:*

The Case for a Liberating Education, and Esmé Raji Codell's book *Educating Esmé*, published in 2000, among many others.

In 1970 the former priest Ivan Illich published *DeSchooling Society*, a book that found its first audience on the left but eventually became a rallying point for the home-schooling movement. Illich argues that most of what goes on in traditional schools has little to do with learning; it reinforces the regimentation and closed-mindedness of a culture that has little room for experimentation or joy in daily life. Illich encourages the habits of lifelong learning and rejects the usefulness of traditional schools as sources of authentic learning.

Sarah Lawrence-Lightfoot, a professor at Harvard's Graduate School of Education, published her book *The Good High School* in 1983. While she does not put forward any particular thesis or program for school improvement, her portraits of successful high schools reveal the human qualities that great schools all share. Roland S. Barthes, a former grade-school principal, published his book *Run, School, Run* in 1980. Like Lawrence-Lightfoot, Barthes avoids theories and prescriptions in his book and simply describes how he ran his school for a decade, emphasizing the small exchanges between teachers, students, and parents that made his school work. A powerful theory of education centering on respect for students and teachers emerges between the lines.

Nineteen eighty-four saw the publication of two important education books, *Horace's Compromise* by Theodore Sizer, and *The Paideia Program* by Mortimer Adler. Both books represent a practical step forward from the thoughtful criticism that dominated education books of the late 1960s and 1970s. Sizer, hinting broadly at Horace Mann in his title, proposes a series of practical steps that teachers and principals can take to bring more freedom and creativity into the classroom while giving students more guidance and better evaluations of their work. He is a strong proponent of small schools and of portfolio-based evaluation of students. Adler, the long-time partner of Robert Maynard Hutchins in the Great Books movement, offers a similarly detailed and practical approach to making education more effective and meaningful. He calls for a division of instruction into three broad categories— direct instruction, seminar-style dialogue, and coaching—and reaffirms Hutchins's insistence on the challenging study of traditional Western texts. Both these books have had enormous impact. Hundreds of schools in the United States are now part of Sizer's Coalition for Essential Schools, and while Adler's followers count only a few dozen certified Paideia schools, many more have informally adopted his model.

In 1995 more than one landmark education book emerged. Maxine Greene's *Releasing the Imagination: Essays on Education, the Arts, and Social Change* crystallizes an important thinker's ideas about the ways that schools connect with other institutions in society. Greene's work builds on Dewey's core notion that school is not preparation for life, but life itself. Deborah Meier's book *The Power of Their Ideas: Lessons for America from a Small School in Harlem* tells the story of her remarkable successes as a principal in a tough New York City school. Meier, a fierce advocate for her students, argues against the district-level structures and practices that address teachers and students only as groups. She believes mightily in the need to address students as individuals, and has long been a colleague and collaborator with Sizer. Lisa Delpit's *Other People's Children* takes a more complicated position on educating minority children. Like Hutchins and Adler, Delpit argues for high academic standards for all children and sees the systematic lowering of expectations for minority children as an expression of structural racism. But she is skeptical about affirming a single canon or curriculum, and argues for recognition of the cultural differences that minority children bring with them into the classroom.

Alfie Kohn emerged in the late 1990s as one of the most important critics of the standardized-testing movement, with two books: *What to Look for in a Classroom, And Other Essays*, published in 1998, and *The Schools Our Children Deserve: Moving Beyond Traditional Classrooms and Tougher Standards*, published in 1999. Kohn argues that too much emphasis on standardized testing obscures the real work of education and drives creativity, spontaneity, and respect for the individual student from the classroom.

The scholar Diane Ravitch published her monumental history of American education reform in 2000. The book, *Left Back*, is also something of a conservative polemic, declaring most reform efforts in American schools in the twentieth century to be failures, and calling for a fairly standard skills-and-facts-based curriculum. But Ravitch claims a radically democratic bias: she believes in a traditional curriculum, she writes, because it is precisely the rigorous, traditional academic path that poor people in the United States are too often denied access to, whether on grounds of bald prejudice or in the name of compassion. Ravitch bases her philosophy on Francis Bacon's famous observation that "Knowledge is power." Ravitch sees too many experimental reforms as diminishing the teacher's role of transmitting knowledge to students and thus helping them become more powerful. Dewey too is a fan of Bacon, but mostly for his pioneering faith in scientific method. Where Dewey sees Bacon as an inspiration for moving experimentation into the center of the school's work, Ravitch seems to disagree. With that disagreement, education books ended the twentieth century on more or less the same note with which they began it.

Index

Index

Index

Index

Index

A NOTE ON THE AUTHOR

Peter Temes was born in Brooklyn, New York, and graduated from the public schools there before studying at the State University of New York at Binghamton. He went on to receive three master's degrees and a Ph.D. from Columbia University, and at age twenty-six joined the faculty of Harvard University. He has since taught at every level of American education, from first grade to graduate school. His first book was *One School Now: Real Life at Lynn English High School*. Mr. Temes is now president of the Great Books Foundation, which helps train teachers and bring the serious discussion of great literature to more than one million students in the United States and abroad. He lives with his wife and three children in Naperville, Illinois.